Marcus Deminco

Marcus Deminco

Translated by Ilka Andrade Suarez
Copyright © 2019 - Marcus Deminco
All Rights Reserved | Salvador – Bahia – Brazil
ISBN: 9781651387221
Independently Published

Formatting, layout and conversion for eBooks
Marlon Bellator
md.bellator@gmail.com
Cover Creation
Erick Cerqueira (Marketing & Design)
http://esc3d.com.br

D395s

Deminco, Marcus

ADHD - Attention Deficit Hyperactivity Disorder. Diagnosing Children and Adults / Marcus Deminco – 1ª ed. – Salvador : Independently Published, 2019. Translated by Ilka Andrade Suarez
Marcus Deminco, 2019.
175 p.

ISBN: 9781651387221

1. Attention Deficit Hyperactivity Disorder. 2. Tests, Scales, Questionnaires, Diagnosis 3. Psychology. I. Title. Diagnosing Children and Adults, ADHD – Attention Deficit Hyperactivity Disorder.
I.,. II. Título.

CDD-658.45
CDU: 811.134.3

Scheda di catalogazione preparata dal sistema bibliotecario universitario (SIBI / UFBA)

ADHD

Attention Deficit Hyperactivity Disorder

Diagnosing

Children and Adults

Marcus Deminco

Marcus Deminco

Translated by Ilka Andrade Suarez
Copyright © 2019 - Marcus Deminco
All Rights Reserved | Salvador – Bahia – Brazil
ISBN: 9781651387221
Independently Published

Marcus Deminco

Summary

Clarification Note

The verb diagnose, derives from the Greek expression's "day", which means "through, during, through" and "gignosko" meaning "knowing, knowing". The definition of the word brought by the Dictionary of the Portuguese Language, conceptualizes diagnosis as the knowledge of a disease through its symptoms, signs and /or various tests. In clinical practice, the diagnosis is usually the result of the analysis performed by observing the symptoms manifested in the present and/or in the past. It is considered the first and most important tool that a health professional establishes to approach the understanding of complaints, and to develop an adequate treatment to the sanitary conditions of his patient.

In this respect, considering that many symptomatic characteristics necessary to determine a diagnosis of Hyperactivity Attention Deficit Disorder (**ADHD**) are equivalent to normal behaviors, it is important to analyze the frequency, duration and persistence of these symptoms in different contexts in the patient's life. Consequently, the use of scales, psychological and neuropsychological tests — as well as the collection of information obtained through specific interviews conducted at school and with family members — serve as valuable sources of information and essential resources to consolidate the diagnosis.

> There is no single test or a battery of tests that allow determining the presence or absence of **ADHD**; therefore, it is a clinical diagnosis that is carried out from the reports of parents and, especially, teachers and neurological evaluation, which allows determining immaturity or changes in the development of the child (CONDEMARÍN et al., 2006).

Therefore, because of its relevance, the main purpose of this book is to make accessible a wide variety of instruments that enable a better assessment of the possibility of Attention Deficit Hyperactivity Disorder (**ADHD**) in children, youth, and adults. However, by no means do the resources available here - albeit of great value - have the character of asserting any diagnosis. It is noteworthy that the diagnosis of **ADHD** is strictly clinical, and no single tool replaces thorough observational analysis and a specific anamnesis performed by a skilled, skilled and experienced professional. It is also important to note that - because much of the content of this book has been translated from other languages - possibly some expressions and / or excerpts appear to have a slight inaccuracy and / or ambiguity of language.

The diagnosis of ADHD by ICD

Published by the World Health Organization (WHO) the International Classification of Diseases and Related Health Problems, generally more recognized by the acronym **ICD** (International Classification of Diseases) — although it is not the most used instrument by mental health professionals in the preparation of diagnoses — also has its importance and purpose. The document provides codes that determine the classification and codification of diseases, and a wide variety of signs, symptoms, unusual aspects, complaints, social circumstances and external causes of damage and/or disease. For each clinical picture a single category is assigned to which a code corresponds, which can contain up to six characters.

Thus, the **ICD** serves as the main information vehicle in identifying trends and statistics of morbidity and mortality worldwide. According to the 10th edition of the International Classification of Diseases (ICD-10), hyperactivity attention deficit disorder (**ADHD**) is part of Hyperkinetic Disorders (F-90).

Hyperkinetic Disorders (F-90) are characterized by early onset (usually during the first five years of life), lack of perseverance in activities that require cognitive involvement, and a tendency to move from one activity to another without ending any, associated with a disorganized, uncoordinated and excessive global activity. Disorders may follow up from other anomalies. Hyperkinetic children are often reckless and impulsive, subject to accidents and incur more disciplinary problems for unpremeditated violations of rules than by deliberate challenge. Their relationships with adults are often marked by an absence of social inhibition, with lack of normal caution and reserve. They are unpopular with other children and can become socially isolated. These disorders are often accompanied by a cognitive deficit and a specific delay in the development of motricity and language. Secondary complications include dissocial behavior and loss of self-esteem.

Hyperkinetic Disorders (F-90) are subdivided into:

1) (F90.0) Activity and attention disorders;

2) (F90.1) Hyperkinetic disorder of conduct;

3) (F90.8) Other hyperkinetic disorders;

4) (F90.9) Unspecified hyperkinetic disorder;

According to the International Classification of Diseases (**ICD-10**) to diagnose a case of **ADHD** it is necessary that the evaluated person presents at least six of the symptoms of inattention and/or six of the symptoms of hyperactivity. In addition, these symptoms should manifest in at least two different environments, and for a period of more than six months.

A. With Predominance of Inattention

The predominance of **CARE** is characterized when the person presents six (or more) of the following persistent symptoms of inattention for at least 6 months, to a poorly adaptive degree and inconsistent with the level of development:

1. It often stops paying attention to detail or makes errors by carelessness in school activities, working among others.

2. He often struggles to keep an eye on tasks or recreational activities.

3. He often doesn't seem to listen when they're addressing his word.

4. It often does not follow instructions and does not terminate your school duties, household chores or professional duties (not due to opposition behavior or inability to understand instructions).

5. It often has difficulty organizing tasks and activities.

6. It often avoids, antipathizes or relutes to engage in tasks that require constant mental effort (such as school tasks or homework).

7. It often loses things necessary for tasks or activities (e.g. toys, school tasks, pencils, books, or other materials).

8. It is easily distracted by stimuli unrelated to the task.

9. It often presents forgetfulness in daily activities.

B. With Predominance of Hyperactivity and/or Impulsivity

It is characterized when six (or more) of the following hyperactivity symptoms persists for at least 6 months, to a poorly adaptive degree and inconsistent with the level of development:

B.1 Hyperactivity

1. It often shakes hands or feet.

2. He often leaves his chair in the classroom or other situations in which he is expected to remain seated.

3. It often runs or scales too much, in situations in which this is inappropriate (in adolescents and adults, it may be limited to subjective sensations of restlessness).

4. He often has difficulty playing or silently engaging in leisure activities.

5. It is often "a thousand" or often acts as if it were "in full swing".

6. He often speaks too much.

B.2 Impulsivity

1. It often gives hasty answers before the questions have been completed.

2. You often have trouble waiting for your turn.

3. Often interrupts or gets into other people's affairs (e.g., intrudes into conversations or jokes).

C. Criteria for both cases

In both cases the following criteria should also be present:

1. Some symptoms of hyperactivity/impulsivity or inattention that caused injury were present before 7 years of age.

2. Any impairment caused by symptoms is present in two or more contexts (e.g. at school, at work and/or at home).

3. There should be clear evidence of clinically significant impairment in social, academic or occupational functioning.

4. Symptoms do not occur exclusively during the course of an invasive developmental disorder, schizophrenia or other psychotic disorder and are no longer well explained by other mental disorder (e.g., mood disorder, anxiety disorder, dissociative disorder, or some personality disorder).

NOTE*: symptoms of inattention, hyperactivity or impulsivity related to the use of medications (such as bronchodilators, isoniazid and neuroleptic a catalyzed) in children under 7 years of age should not be diagnosed as **ADHD.**

The diagnosis of ADHD by DSM

The *Diagnostic and Statistical Manual of Mental Disorders*, better known by the acronym **DSM** is a manual for mental health professionals who lists different categories of mental disorders and criteria for diagnosing them. Prepared by the *American Psychiatric Association* (APA) currently represents the best clinical use tool to diagnose mental disorders-related conditions and has been one of the most widely used sources for mental health diagnoses worldwide.

In its 5th review, **DSM-V** classifies Attention Deficit Hyperactivity Disorder **(ADHD)** among Neurodevelopmental Disorders. Neurodevelopmental Disorders correspond to a group with beginning, usually manifested before the child enters school, being characterized by developmental deficits that result in impairments in personal, social, academic and/or professional functioning. Development deficits range from specific limitations in learning and/or controlling executive functions to triggering serious global damage in social skills or intelligence. There is also frequent the simultaneous presence of more than one disorder during the course of the individual diagnosed with some Neurodevelopmental

Disorder. For example, individuals with Autism Spectrum Disorder (**ASD**) often have Intellectual Development Disorder (**TDI**). While many children with Attention Deficit Hyperactivity Disorder (**ADHD**) commonly have comorbidity with some Specific Learning Disorder.

ADHD is a Neurodevelopmental Disorder defined by harmful levels of inattention, disorganization and/or hyperactivity-impulsivity. **(a)** Inattention and disorganization involve inability to remain on a task, appearance of not listening, and loss of materials at levels inconsistent with age or level of development. **(b)** Hyperactivity-impulsivity implies excessive activities, restlessness, inability to remain seated and/or in the same position and/or place. They also have meddling in other people's activities and inability to wait —symptoms that are excessive for age or level of development. In childhood, **ADHD** often overlaps with disorders in general considered "extremization", such as challenging opposition disorder and conduct disorder. **ADHD** usually persists in adulthood, resulting in losses in social, academic and professional functioning.

ADHD - Diagnostic Criteria (DSM-V)

A. A persistent pattern of inattention and/or hyperactivity-impulsivity that interferes with functioning and development, as characterized by **(1)** and/or **(2)**:

1. Inattention: Six (or more) of the following symptoms persist for at least six months to a degree that is inconsistent with the level of development and causes negative impact directly on social and academic/professional activities:

NOTE*: Symptoms are not just a manifestation of opposing behavior, challenge, hostility or difficulty in understanding tasks or instructions. For older adolescents and adults (17 years or older), at least five symptoms are needed.

a) He often pays no attention in detail or makes errors by carelessness in school tasks, at work or during other activities (e.g. neglects or lets details pass, work is inaccurate).

b) It often has difficulty keeping an eye on recreational tasks or activities (e.g., difficulty staying focused during classes, conversations, or prolonged readings).

c) He often seems not to listen when someone directs his word directly (e.g. he seems to be away with his head, even in the absence of any obvious distraction).

d) It often does not follow instructions to the end and cannot finish schoolwork, tasks or duties in the workplace (e.g. begins tasks, but quickly loses focus and easily loses course).

e) Often it has difficulty organizing tasks and activities (e.g., difficulty managing sequential tasks; difficulty keeping materials and personal objects in order; disorganized and sloppy work; poor weather management; difficulty in meeting deadlines).

f) It often avoids, dislikes or relutes in engaging in tasks that require prolonged mental effort (e.g. schoolwork or homework;

for older adolescents and adults, preparing reports, filling out forms, reviewing long works).

g) Often loses things necessary for tasks or activities (e.g. school materials, pencils, books, instruments, wallets, keys, documents, glasses, cell phone).

h) It is often easily distracted by external stimuli (for older adolescents and adults, it may include unrelated thoughts).

i) It is often forgotten in relation to daily activities (e.g., performing tasks, obligations; for older adolescents and adults, returning calls, paying bills, keeping schedules scheduled).

2. Hyperactivity and Impulsivity: Six (or more) of the following symptoms persist for at least six months to a degree that is inconsistent with the level of development and generates negative impact directly on social and academic/professional activities:

NOTE*: Symptoms are not just a manifestation of opposing behavior, challenge, hostility or difficulty understanding tasks or instructions. For older adolescents and adults (17 years or older), at least five symptoms are needed.

---

a) Often stir or batuca the hands or feet or writhe in the chair.

b) He often raises his chair in situations where he is expected to remain seated (e.g. he leaves his place in the classroom, in the office or in another workplace or in other situations that require him to remain in the same place).

c) It often runs or climbs things in situations where this is inappropriate. (Note: In adolescents or adults, it may be limited to feelings of restlessness.)

d) He is often unable to play or engage in leisure activities quietly.

e) Often "does not stop", acting as if "with the engine on" (e.g. can't or feel uncomfortable standing still for a long time, such as in restaurants, meetings; others can see the individual as restless or difficult to keep up).

f) He often talks too much.

g) Often misses an answer before the question has been completed (e.g. ends other people's sentences, cannot wait for the turn to speak).

h) You often have difficulty waiting for your turn (e.g. waiting in a queue).

i) Often interrupts or meddles (e.g. get into conversations, games or activities; you can start using other people's things without asking or receiving permission; for teenagers and adults, you can step into or take control over what others are doing).

B. Several symptoms of inattention or hyperactivity-impulsivity were present before the age of 12.

C. Several symptoms of inattention or hyperactivity-impulsivity are present in two or more environments (e.g. at home, at school, at work; with friends or relatives; in other activities).

D. There is clear evidence that symptoms interfere with social, academic or professional functioning or that they reduce their quality.

E. Symptoms do not occur exclusively during the course of schizophrenia or other psychotic disorder and are no longer well explained by other mental disorder (e.g., mood disorder, anxiety disorder, dissociative disorder, personality, intoxication or abstinence of substance).

Determine subtype:

- 314.1 (F90.2) Combined presentation: If both Criterion A1 (inattention) and Criterion A2 (hyperactivity-impulsivity) are completed in the last 6 months.

- 314.0 (F90.0) Predominantly inattentive presentation: If Criterion A1 (inattention) is met, but Criterion A2 (hyperactivity-impulsivity) is not completed in the last 6 months.

- 314.1 (F90.1) Predominantly overactive/impulsive presentation: If Criterion A2 (hyperactivity-impulsivity) is met, and Criterion A1 (inattention) is not completed in the last 6 months.

Specify whether:

In partial remission: When all criteria have been met in the past, but not all criteria have been met in the last 6 months. However, symptoms still result in impairment in social, academic or professional functioning.

Specify the current severity:

1. **Mild**: Few symptoms, if any are present, in addition to those necessary to make the diagnosis, and symptoms result in no more than minor impairments in social or professional functioning.

2. **Moderate**: Symptoms or functional impairment between "mild" and "severe" are present.

3. **Severe**: Many symptoms beyond those necessary to make the diagnosis are present, or several particularly severe symptoms are present, or symptoms can result in marked impairment in social or professional functioning.

Diagnostic Characteristics

The essential characteristic of Attention Deficit Hyperactivity Disorder is a persistent pattern of Inattention and/or Hyperactivity-Impulsivity that interferes with functioning or development. **INATTENTION** manifests itself through ramblings in tasks, lack of persistence, difficulty maintaining focus and disorganization - and does not constitute a consequence of challenge or lack of understanding. **HYPERACTIVITY** refers to excessive motor activity (such as a child running for everything) when not appropriate or rummaging, hitting or chatting in excess. In adults, hyperactivity may manifest itself as extreme restlessness or exhaustion of others with their activity. **IMPULSIVITY** refers to hasty actions that occur at the moment without premeditation and with high potential for harm to the person (e.g., crossing a street without looking). **IMPULSIVITY** may be a reflection of a desire for immediate rewards or inability to postpone gratification. Impulsive behavior may manifest with social meddling (e.g. interrupting others in excess) and/or making important decisions without considerations about the long-term consequences (e.g. taking a job without adequate information).

ADHD begins in childhood. The requirement that several symptoms be present before the age of 12 expresses the importance of substantial clinical presentation during childhood. At the same time, an earlier onset age is not specified due to difficulties in retrospectively establishing an onset in childhood. Adult memories of childhood symptoms tend to be unreliable, and it is beneficial to obtain complementary information.

Manifestations of the disorder should be present in more than one environment (e.g. at home and at school, at work). Confirmation of substantial symptoms in various environments is not usually done accurately without a consultation with informants who have seen the individual in such environments. Symptoms vary by context in a given environment. Signs of the disorder can be minimal or absent when the individual is receiving frequent rewards for appropriate behavior, is under supervision, is in a new situation, is involved in especially interesting activities, receives consistent external stimuli (e.g. through electronic screens) or are interacting in individualized situations (e.g. in an office).

Associated Characteristics That Support Diagnosis

Mild delays in linguistic, motor or social development are not specific to **ADHD,** although they are usually comorbid. Associated characteristics may include low tolerance to frustration, irritability, or mood lability. Even in the absence of a specific learning disorder, academic or professional performance is usually impaired. Inattentive behavior is associated with several underlying cognitive processes, and individuals with **ADHD** may exhibit cognitive problems in attention tests, executive function, or memory, although these tests are not sensitive enough or specific enough to serve as diagnostic indices. At the beginning of adulthood, **ADHD** is associated with increased risk of suicide attempt, especially when comorbidity with mood, conduct or substance use disorders.

There is no biological marker that is diagnosed with **ADHD.** As a group, in the comparison with pairs, children with **ADHD** present electroencephalograms with increased slow waves, reduced total brain volume in magnetic resonance imaging and possibly delay in cortical maturation in the postretirees anterior sense, although these findings are not diagnostic. In rare cases where there is a known genetic cause (e.g., Fragile X syndrome, 22q11 deletion syndrome), the presentation of **ADHD** should still be diagnosed.

Prevalence

Population surveys suggest that **ADHD** occurs in most cultures in about 5% of children and 2.5% of adults.

Development and Course

Many parents observe for the first-time excessive motor activity when the child begins to walk, but it is difficult to distinguish the symptoms of normal behavior, which is highly variable, before 4 years of age. **ADHD** is usually identified more frequently during the years of elementary school, with inattention becoming more salient and harmful. The disorder becomes relatively stable in the early years of adolescence, but some individuals have worsened in the course, with the development of antisocial behaviors. In most people with **ADHD,** symptoms of motor hyperactivity are less clear in adolescence and adulthood, although difficulties persist with planning, restlessness, inattention and impulsivity. A substantial proportion of children with **ADHD** remain relatively impaired until adulthood.

In preschool, the main manifestation is hyperactivity. Inattention is more prominent in the years of elementary school. In adolescence, signs of hyperactivity (e.g., running and climbing things) are less common, and may be limited to more restless behavior or internal sensation of nervousness, restlessness or impatience. In adulthood, in addition to inattention and restlessness, impulsivity can remain problematic, even when hyperactivity was reduced.

Risk and Prognosis Factors

Temperamental. ADHD is associated with lower levels of behavioral inhibition, stress-based control or containment, negative affectivity and/or greater search for novelties. These traits predispose some children to **ADHD,** although they are not specific to the disorder.

Environmental. Very low birth weight (less than 1,500 grams) confers a 2 to 3 times higher risk for **ADHD,** although most children with low birth weight do not develop disorder. Although **ADHD** is correlated with smoking during pregnancy, part of this association reflects a common genetic risk. A minority of cases may be related to reactions to aspects of diet. There may be a history of child abuse, neglect, multiple foster homes, exposure to neurotoxin (e.g. lead), infections (e.g. encephalitis) or exposure to alcohol in the uterus. Exposure to environmental toxins has been correlated with subsequent **ADHD,** although it is not known whether such associations are causal.

Genetic and physiological. ADHD is frequent in first-degree biological relatives with the disorder. The heritability of **ADHD** is substantial. While specific genes have been correlated with the disorder, they do not constitute necessary or sufficient causal factors. Visual and auditory deficiencies, metabolic abnormalities, sleep disorders, nutritional deficiencies and epilepsy should be considered possible influences on **ADHD** symptoms.

ADHD is not associated with specific physical characteristics, although lower physical abnormalities rates (e.g., hypertelorism, rather arched palate, low ear implantation) may be relatively increased. Subtle motor delays and other mild neurological signs may occur. Note that lack of manner and comorbid engine delays should be coded separately (e.g. coordination development disorder).

Course modifiers. Patterns of family interaction early childhood probably do not cause **ADHD,** although they may influence their course or contribute to the secondary development of conduct problems.

Diagnostic Issues Related to Culture

Regional differences in **ADHD** prevalence rates seem mainly attributable to different diagnostic and methodological practices. However, there may also be cultural variations in terms of attitudes or interpretations about child behavior. Clinical identification rates in the United States for African American and Latin populations tend to be lower than for white populations. Symptom scores by informants may be influenced by the child's and informant's cultural group, suggesting that culturally appropriate practices are relevant in the evaluation of **ADHD.**

Diagnostic Issues Related to Gender

ADHD is more frequent in males than in females in the general population, with a ratio of about 2:1 in children and 1.6:1 in adults. Women are more likely to present themselves primarily with inattention characteristics compared to males.

Functional Consequences of ADHD

ADHD is associated with reduced school performance and academic success, social rejection and, in adults, worse performances, success and attendance in the professional field and the higher probability of unemployment, as well as high levels of interpersonal conflict. Children with **ADHD** are significantly more likely than their peers to develop conduct disorder in adolescence and antisocial personality disorder in adulthood, thereby increasing the likelihood of substance use and imprisonment disorders. The subsequent risk for posterior substance use disorders is high, especially when conduct disorder or antisocial personality disorder develops. Individuals with **ADHD** are more likely to suffer injuries than their peers. Traffic accidents and violations are more frequent in drivers with the disorder. There may be increased probability of obesity among individuals with **ADHD.**

Variable or inadequate self-determination to perform tasks that require prolonged effort is often interpreted by others, such as laziness, irresponsibility or lack of cooperation. Family relationships can be characterized by discord and negative interactions.

Relationships with peers are usually troubled due to rejection by those, neglect or taunts in relation to the individual with **ADHD.** On average, people with the disorder achieve lower schooling, less professional success and reduced intellectual scores compared to their peers, although there is great variability. In its severe form, the disorder is markedly harmful, affecting social, family and school/professional adaptation.

Academic deficits, school problems and neglect by colleagues tend to be mainly associated with high symptoms of inattention, while rejection by colleagues and, to a lesser extent, accidental injuries are more prominent with marked symptoms hyperactivity or impulsivity.

Differential Diagnosis

Defiant Opposition Disorder (TOD). Individuals with challenging opposition disorder can resist professional or school tasks that require self-determination because they resist conforming to the demands of others. His behavior is characterized by negativity, hostility and challenge. Such symptoms should be differentiated from aversion to school or to high-mental requirements tasks caused by difficulty in maintaining prolonged mental exertion, forgetting guidance and impulsivity that characterizes individuals with **ADHD.** A complicating differential diagnosis pain is the fact that some individuals with **ADHD** may develop secondary opposition attitudes towards such tasks and thus devalue their importance.

Intermittent Explosive Disorder (TEI). **ADHD** and intermittent explosive disorder share high levels of impulsive behavior. However, individuals with intermittent explosive disorder present important aggressiveness directed to others, which is not characteristic of **ADHD,** and have no problems keeping attention as seen in **ADHD.** In addition, intermittent explosive disorder is rare in childhood. Intermittent explosive disorder can be diagnosed in the presence of **ADHD.**

Other Neurodevelopmental Disorders. Increased motor activity that may occur in **ADHD** should be differentiated from repetitive motor behavior that characterizes stereotyped movement disorder and some cases of autism spectrum disorder. In stereotyped movement disorder, motor behavior is usually fixed and repetitive (e.g., shaking the body, biting itself), while restlessness and agitation in **ADHD** are usually generalized and not characterized by repetitive stereotyped movements. No; Tourette disorder, multiple and frequent tics can be confused with the widespread restlessness of **ADHD.** There may be a need for prolonged observation in order to distinguish between restlessness and multi-tic attacks.

Specific Learning Disorder (ASAs). Children with a specific learning disorder may seem unattentive due to frustration, lack of interest or limited capacity. Inattention, however, in people with a specific learning disorder, but without **ADHD,** does not cause harm outside of academic work.

Intellectual Disability (Intellectual Development Disorder). ADHD symptoms are common among children placed in academic environments unsuitable for their intellectual capacity. In such cases, symptoms are not evident during non-academic tasks. A diagnosis of **ADHD** in intellectual disability requires that inattention or hyperactivity be excessive for mental age.

Autism Spectrum Disorder (ASAs). Individuals with **ADHD** and those with autism spectrum disorder exhibit inattention, social dysfunction and difficult-to-manage behavior. Social dysfunction and peer rejection found in people with **ADHD** should be differentiated from the lack of social involvement, isolation and indifference to facial and tone communication cues found in individuals with autism spectrum disorder. Children with autism spectrum disorder may have rabies attacks due to the inability to tolerate changes in the course of events expected by them. In contrast, children with **ADHD** can misbehave or have an attack of anger during some major transition due to impulsivity or unsatisfactory self-control.

Reactive Attachment Disorder (ART). Children with reactive attachment disorder may present social disinhibition, but not the complete set of **ADHD** symptoms, exhibiting other characteristics such as absence of lasting relationships, which are not characteristic of **ADHD.**

Anxiety Disorders. **ADHD** shares symptoms of inattention with anxiety disorders. Individuals with **ADHD** are inattentive because of their attraction to external stimuli, new activities or predilection for pleasant activities. This is different from the inattention due to concern and rumination found in anxiety disorders. Agitation can be found in anxiety disorders. In **ADHD,** however, the symptom is not associated with concern and rumination.

Depressive Disorders. Individuals with depressive disorders may present with inability to concentrate. However, the difficulty of concentration in mood disorders is prominent only during a depressive episode.

Bipolar Disorder. Individuals with bipolar disorder may have increased activity, difficulty concentrating and increased impulsivity. These characteristics, however, are episodic, occurring for several days at a time. In bipolar disorder, increased impulsivity or inattention is accompanied by high mood, grandeur and other specific bipolar characteristics. Children with **ADHD** may present important mood swings in the same day; this lability is different from a manic episode, which should last four days or more to be a clinical indicator of bipolar disorder, even in children. Bipolar disorder is rare in pre-adolescents, even when severe irritability and rabies are prominent, while **ADHD** is common among children and adolescents who have excessive rabies and irritability.

Disruptive Mood Dysregulation Disorder. Disruptive mood deregulation disorder is characterized by pervasive irritability and frustration intolerance, but impulsivity and disorganized attention are not essential aspects. Most children and adolescents with the disorder, however, have symptoms that also meet criteria for **ADHD,** which should be diagnosed separately.

Substance Use Disorder (SUD). Differentiating **ADHD** from substance use disorders may be a problem if the first presentation of **ADHD** symptoms occurs after the onset of abuse or frequent use. Clear evidence of **ADHD** prior to problematic substance use, obtained through informants or previous records, may be essential for differential diagnosis.

Personality Disorders. In adolescents and adults, it can be difficult to differentiate **ADHD** from *Borderline personality* disorders, narcissist and other personality disorders. All of these tend to share characteristics of disorganization, social intrusion, emotional deregulation and cognitive deregulation. **ADHD,** however, is not characterized by fear of abandonment, self-injury, extreme ambivalence or other characteristics of personality disorders. There may be a need for prolonged observation, interviews with informants or detailed history to distinguish impulsive, socially intrusive or inadequate behavior from narcissistic, aggressive or dominating behavior in order to make this differential diagnosis.

Psychotic Disorders. **ADHD** is not diagnosed if symptoms of inattention and hyperactivity occur exclusively during the course of a psychotic disorder.

Symptoms of drug-induced ADHD. Symptoms of inattention, hyperactivity or impulsivity attributable to the use of medications (e.g. bronchodilators, isoniazid, neuroleptics [resulting in akathisia], thyroid replacement therapy) are diagnosed as disorder for the use of another substance (or unknown substance) or disorder related to another substance (or unknown substance not specified).

Neurocognitive Disorders. It is not known whether Early Major Neurocognitive Disorder (dementia) and/or Mild Neurocognitive Disorder are associated with **ADHD,** although similar clinical characteristics may often present. These conditions are differentiated from **ADHD** by its late onset.

Comorbidity

In clinical environments, comorbid disorders are frequent in individuals whose symptoms meet criteria for **ADHD.** In the general population, Defiant Opposition Disorder (TOD) is comorbid with **ADHD** in about half of the children with the combined presentation and in about a quarter of those with the predominantly inattentive presentation. Conduct Disorder is comorbid with **ADHD** in approximately a quarter of children and adolescents with combined presentation, depending on age and environment.

Most children and adolescents with Disruptive Mood Deregulation Disorder have symptoms that also meet criteria for **ADHD;** a smaller percentage of children with **ADHD** have symptoms that meet criteria for Disruptive Mood Deregulation Disorder. Specific Learning Disorder (ASD) is commonly comorbid with **ADHD*** Anxiety Disorders and Major Depressive Disorder (TDM) occur in a minority of individuals with **ADHD,** although more frequently than in the general population. Intermittent Explosive Disorder (TEI) occurs in a minority of adults with **ADHD,** although with rates above population levels.

Although substance abuse disorders are relatively more frequent among adults with **ADHD** in the general population, only one minority of them are present. In adults, Antisocial Personality Disorder (TPA) and other personality disorders can be comorbid with **ADHD.** Other disorders that may be comorbid with **ADHD** include Obsessive-Compulsive Disorder (OCD), Tic Disorders, and Autism Spectrum Disorder (ASD).

Other Instruments for Diagnosing ADHD

The evaluation process for the diagnosis of Attention Deficit/Hyperactivity Disorder **(ADHD)** should be carried out through a thorough clinical investigation, contemplating all patient history. However, the more careful this evaluation is performed in relation to the use of instrumental resources, the lower the possibility of making a misunderstanding in the diagnosis. An assessment that — in addition to providing an accurate diagnosis — is able to point out the presence of comorbid disorders, analyzing a perspective on the harmful and misfit functioning of the subject, will also provide a better choice related to the more efficient techniques and/or strategies to be used during their treatment. Thus, favoring the prognosis of the individual.

Thus, although the characteristics present in the International Classification of Diseases **(ICD)** and, above all, the Diagnostic Criteria described in the Diagnostic and Statistical Manual of Mental Disorders **(DSM)** are considered as the most reliable and consistent instruments to assist in the diagnosis process of **ADHD,** there is a wide variety of tests, scales and other psychological instruments that may, and should be used in order to corroborate the accuracy in the evaluation process and diagnosis of Attention Deficit Hyperactivity Disorder **(ADHD).**

SNAP-IV — For ADHD Diagnosis in Children and Adolescents

Public domain tool, the Swanson Nolan and Pelham-IV Questionnaire, or simply SNAP-IV is an easy-to-use questionnaire, was developed from the same criteria present in **DSM** to assess the symptoms of Attention Deficit Hyperactivity Disorder (ADHD) in children and adolescents. Because the characteristics of **ADHD** usually manifest themselves in different contexts, this questionnaire can also be completed by parents and/or teachers.

How to Use

For each of the **18** sentences described below choice and mark one of the **4** answer options that best corresponds to the child or adolescent evaluated.

1. You cannot pay much attention to detail or make mistakes for carelessness in schoolwork or chores.

( ) Not a little
( ) Just a little
( ) Quite
( ) Too much

2. You have difficulty keeping an eye on leisure tasks or activities.

( ) Not a little
( ) Just a little
( ) Quite

( ) Too much

3. You don't seem to be listening when you talk to him directly.

( ) Not a little
( ) Just a little
( ) Quite
( ) Too much

4. Do not follow instructions to the end and does not terminate school duties, tasks or obligations.

( ) Not a little
( ) Just a little
( ) Quite
( ) Too much

5. Have difficulty organizing tasks and activities.

( ) Not a little
( ) Just a little
( ) Quite
( ) Too much

6. Avoids, dislikes or engages against will in tasks that require prolonged mental effort.

( ) Not a little
( ) Just a little
( ) Quite
( ) Too much

7. Loses things necessary for activities (e.g. toys, school duties, pencils or books).

( ) Not a little
( ) Just a little
( ) Quite
( ) Too much

8. Get distracted by external stimuli.

( ) Not a little
( ) Just a little
( ) Quite
( ) Too much

9. It is forgotten in day-to-day activities.

( ) Not a little
( ) Just a little
( ) Quite
( ) Too much

10. Stir with your hands, feet or stir in the chair.

( ) Not a little
( ) Just a little
( ) Quite
( ) Too much

11. You leave the place in the classroom or in other situations where you are expected to sit (a).

( ) Not a little
( ) Just a little

( ) Quite
( ) Too much

12. Runs from side to side or climbs things in inappropriate situations.

( ) Not a little
( ) Just a little
( ) Quite
( ) Too much

13. Demonstrates difficulty in playing or engaging in leisure activities in a quiet way.

( ) Not a little
( ) Just a little
( ) Quite
( ) Too much

14. Not quiet or often is "a thousand per hour".

( ) Not a little
( ) Just a little
( ) Quite
( ) Too much

15. You talk too much.

( ) Not a little
( ) Just a little
( ) Quite
( ) Too much

16. Answer questions hastily before they are even completed.

( ) Not a little
( ) Just a little
( ) Quite
( ) Too much

17. Finds it difficult to wait for your turn.

( ) Not a little
( ) Just a little
( ) Quite
( ) Too much

18. Stop others or intrude in conversations, games, etc.

( ) Not a little
( ) Just a little
( ) Quite
( ) Too much

How to Evaluate

1. If at least 6 items were marked as **QUITE** or **TOO MUCH** from 1 to 9 = there are more symptoms of inattention than expected for a child or adolescent.

2. If at least 6 items were marked as **QUITE** or **TOO MUCH** from 10 to 18 = there are more symptoms of hyperactivity and impulsivity than expected for a child or adolescent.

IMPORTANT: You cannot diagnose **ADHD** only with criterion A. Therefore, to consider the diagnosis see below the other criteria that are also needed.

Criterion A: Symptoms (seen above)

Criterion B: Some of these symptoms should be present before 7 years of age.

Criterion C: There are problems caused by the above symptoms in at least 2 different contexts (e.g. at school, at work, social life and at home).

Criterion D: There are obvious problems in school, social or family life due to symptoms.

Criterion E: If there is any other problem (such as depression, mental deficiency, psychosis, etc.), symptoms cannot be attributed exclusively to it.

ASRS-18 - For the Diagnosis of ADHD in Adults

The Adult Self-Report Scale (ASRS-18) is an important tool to aid in the diagnosis of **ADHD** in adults. The scale was developed by researchers in collaboration with the World Health Organization (WHO) and validated for the Portuguese language in 2006. Considering that certain symptoms appear more strongly in specific environments such as work, at home or leisure, the scale is also recommended for it to be filled both by the patient and his/her family members, co-workers and/or friends.

The scale has 18 items that contemplate the symptoms present in **Criterion A** of the **DSM.** However, modified and adapted to the context of adult life. And it offers 5 different scores for each frequency response option:

1. **Never = 0 Points**
2. **Rarely = 1 Point**
3. **Sometimes = 2 Points**
4. **Often = 3 Points**
5. **Very Often = 4 Points**

How to Use

Answer the questions below according to the score the frequency answer options that best represent how the person evaluated felt and/or behaved in the last six months.

PART A

1. How often do you make mistakes for lack of attention when you have to work on a boring or difficult project?

( ) Never

( ) Rarely

( ) Sometimes

( ) Often

( ) Very Often

2. How often do you have difficulty keeping an eye out when you are doing a boring or repetitive job?

( ) Never

( ) Rarely

( ) Sometimes

( ) Often

( ) Very Often

3. How often do you have difficulty focusing on what people say, even when they are talking directly to you?

( ) Never

( ) Rarely

( ) Sometimes

( ) Often

( ) Very Often

4. How often do you leave a project in half after you have already made the most difficult parts?

( ) Never

( ) Rarely

( ) Sometimes

( ) Often

( ) Very Often

5. How often do you have difficulty doing a job that requires organization?

( ) Never

( ) Rarely

( ) Sometimes

( ) Often

( ) Very Often

6. When you need to do something that requires a lot of concentration, with what frequência you avoid or postpone the beginning?

( ) Never

( ) Rarely

( ) Sometimes

( ) Often

( ) Very Often

7. How often do you put things out of place or have difficulty finding things at home or at work?

( ) Never

( ) Rarely

( ) Sometimes

( ) Often

( ) Very Often

8. How often do you get distracted by aividades or noise around you?

( ) Never

( ) Rarely

( ) Sometimes

( ) Often

( ) Very Often

9. How often do you have difficulty remembering appointments or obligations?

( ) Never

( ) Rarely

( ) Sometimes

( ) Often

( ) Very Often

PART B

1. How often do you keep moving in the chair or shaking your hands or feet when you need to sit (a) for a long time?

( ) Never

( ) Rarely

( ) Sometimes

( ) Often

( ) Very Often

2. How often do you get up from the chair in meetings or in other situations where you should sit (a)?

( ) Never

( ) Rarely

( ) Sometimes

( ) Often

( ) Very Often

3. How often do you feel restless (a) or agitated(a)?

( ) Never

( ) Rarely

( ) Sometimes

( ) Often

( ) Very Often

4. How often do you have difficulty settle down and relax when you have free time?

( ) Never

( ) Rarely

( ) Sometimes

( ) Often

( ) Very Often

5. How often do you feel too active and needing to do things, like you're "with an engine turned on"?

( ) Never

( ) Rarely

( ) Sometimes

( ) Often

( ) Very Often

6. How often do you get too much falanin social situations?

( ) Never

( ) Rarely

( ) Sometimes

( ) Often

( ) Very Often

7. When you're talking, how often do you catch yourself by finishing people's sentences before them?

( ) Never

( ) Rarely

( ) Sometimes

( ) Often

( ) Very Often

8. How often do you have difficulty waiting in situations where each one has his turn?

( ) Never

( ) Rarely

( ) Sometimes

( ) Often

( ) Very Often

9. How often do you interrupt others when they are busy?

( ) Never

( ) Rarely

( ) Sometimes

( ) Often

( ) Very Often

How to Evaluate

If the items of inattention of part A (1 to 9) and/or the items of hyperactivity-impulsivity of part B (1 to 9) have several answers marked **OFTEN** or **VERY OFTEN** there is a great chance that the evaluated person is carrier that of **ADHD** (at least 4 in each of the parts).

IMPORTANT: cannot diagnose **ADHD** only with the symptoms shown in the table. To consider the diagnosis see below the other criteria that are also required.

Criterion A: Symptoms (seen in the table above)

Criterion B: Some of these symptoms should be present from an early age (up to 12 years).

Criterion C: There are problems caused by the above symptoms in at least 2 different contexts (e.g. at work, social life, college and marital or family relationships).

Criterion D: There are obvious problems due to symptoms.

Criterion E: If there is the presence of any other disorder (such as depression, mental deficiency, psychosis, etc.), symptoms cannot be attributed exclusively to it.

NOTE*: The American study that originated the creation of ASRS-18 suggests that a score above 24 is considered as a strong indication for the presence of **ADHD** in adults. However, it is essential to confirm attested by a specialist, considering that many of the symptoms described in the scale may be associated with other comorbidities related to **ADHD** and/or other psychopathological conditions.

Preliminary Assessment Criteria for ADHD in Adults

This test is based on the list of symptoms that characterize Attention Deficit Hyperactivity Disorder (**ADHD**) in its adult manifestation. However, its assessment should only be considered as a secondary resource for the indication of **ADHD**.

How to Use

Check in the table below, the options that best refer to the person evaluated. In the end, the more alternatives are marked, the greater the probability of the presence of **ADHD.**

Inattentive Type

(1) Pay little attention to detail and usually makes mistakes due to lack of attention.

(2) You have trouble concentrating when watching a lecture, reading a book, etc.

(3) Sometimes you don't seem to hear when they're being directed at you, or in a conversation you end up paying attention to other things.

(4) He has difficulty following the instructions (not because of inability to understand them), always preferring to do his tasks "in his own way", in "his time", often leaving them unfinished.

(5) Difficulty organizing your time to do something or plan something in advance.

(6) Reluctance to do or initiate tasks that require mental and constant effort for a long time.

(7) Loses objects and/or forgets names, appointments, dates.

(8) Easily distract yourself with things around you or even with your own thoughts, often appearing to "dream awake".

(9) It often presents forgetfulness in its daily activities.

It is necessary that the person has 5 or more of the above symptoms, in order to be more likely to diagnose ADHD of the Inattentive Type.

Hyperactive / Impulsive Type

(1) The feet, hands or stirs in the chair incessantly.

(2) You have difficulty sitting (a) in situations where this is expected.

(3) He feels unable to relax, rest, the musculature is usually tense and is always in search of something to do.

(4) He has difficulty staying silent in leisure activities.

(5) It seems to be powered by an "electric" engine, as it is always, the "thousand per hour".

(6) Talk, eat, buy or work too hard.

(7) He hastily answers questions before they are completed. Answer written questions before reading to the end.

(8) You have difficulty waiting your turn: in conversations, queues, restaurants.

(9) Often interrupt others in your activities and/or conversations.

It is necessary that the person has 5 or more symptoms to have a greater possibility of the diagnosis of Hyperactive/Impulsive ADHD.

Combined Type

It is necessary that the person has 5 or more symptoms of each of the above 2 groups for greater possibility of diagnosis of Combined Type ADHD.

IMPORTANT! In the diagnosis of **ADHD,** in addition to the above symptoms, the other criteria should also be observed:

A. Symptoms   (seen above).

B. Some of these symptoms should be present before 12 years of age.

C. There are problems caused by the above symptoms in at least 2 different contexts (work, in social life, college, marital and/or family relationship).

D. There are obvious problems in professional, social, family and/or affective life due to symptoms.

E. If there is another problem (such as depression, mental deficiency, psychosis, etc.), symptoms cannot be attributed exclusively to it.

ADHD — Screening Quiz for Adults

Developed in the early 1990s by Larry Jasper and Ivan Goldberg, ADHD — Screening Quiz for Adults is a screening assessment to verify the existence of **ADHD** in adults.

How to Use

The 24 items proposed below should be in harmony with how the appraised person behaved and felt for most of their adult life. If it has been generally one way but has recently changed, your answers should follow the reflection: "How Has This Person Been Generally?" Then, for each question presented, consider 1 of the 6 answers below that best matches the person evaluated.

1. **Never = 0 Points**
2. **Just A Little = 1 Point**
3. **Reasonably = 2 Points**
4. **Moderately = 3 Points**
5. **Most of the time = 4 Points**
6. **Very = 5 Points**

1. At home, at work or at school, I feel my mind moving away from uninteresting or difficult tasks.

( ) Never
( ) Just a little
( ) Reasonably
( ) Moderately
( ) Most of the time
( ) Very

2. I find it difficult to read written texts unless it's about something very interesting and/or very easy to read.

( ) Never
( ) Just a little
( ) Reasonably
( ) Moderately
( ) Most of the time
( ) Very

3. Especially in groups, I find it difficult to stay focused (a) on what is being said in the conversations.

( ) Never
( ) Just a little
( ) Reasonably
( ) Moderately
( ) Most of the time
( ) Very

4. I have an cranky temper and i'm usually "short wick."

( ) Never
( ) Just a little
( ) Reasonably
( ) Moderately
( ) Most of the time
( ) Very

5. I get angry easily and i get bored for little things.

( ) Never
( ) Just a little
( ) Reasonably
( ) Moderately

( ) Most of the time
( ) Very

6. Often, I say things without thinking, and then I regret saying them.

( ) Never
( ) Just a little
( ) Reasonably
( ) Moderately
( ) Most of the time
( ) Very

7. I generally make hasty decisions without assessing enough about its possible consequences.

( ) Never
( ) Just a little
( ) Reasonably
( ) Moderately
( ) Most of the time
( ) Very

8. I have problems in interpersonal relationships due to my tendency to speak first and think afterwards.

( ) Never
( ) Just a little
( ) Reasonably
( ) Moderately
( ) Most of the time
( ) Very

9. My mood oscillates from one end to the other, between ups and downs.

( ) Never
( ) Just a little
( ) Reasonably
( ) Moderately
( ) Most of the time
( ) Very

10. I have difficulty planning on what order should I follow to perform the tasks or activities.

( ) Never
( ) Just a little
( ) Reasonably
( ) Moderately
( ) Most of the time
( ) Very

11. I get bored (a) with ease.

( ) Never
( ) Just a little
( ) Reasonably
( ) Moderately
( ) Most of the time
( ) Very

12. I have low tolerance for negative reviews, and I am easily upset about it.

( ) Never
( ) Just a little
( ) Reasonably

( ) Moderately
( ) Most of the time
( ) Very

13. I'm almost always moving. I'm very agitated.

( ) Never
( ) Just a little
( ) Reasonably
( ) Moderately
( ) Most of the time
( ) Very

14. I feel more comfortable when I'm moving, than when I'm standing.

( ) Never
( ) Just a little
( ) Reasonably
( ) Moderately
( ) Most of the time
( ) Very

15. In conversations, I begin to answer the questions even before people formulate it entirely.

( ) Never
( ) Just a little
( ) Reasonably
( ) Moderately
( ) Most of the time
( ) Very

16. I usually work on more than one project at the same time, and normally, I end up not completing many of them.

( ) Never
( ) Just a little
( ) Reasonably
( ) Moderately
( ) Most of the time
( ) Very

17. There are always many internal ideas, thoughts and dialogues in my head, as a kind of "chatter".

( ) Never
( ) Just a little
( ) Reasonably
( ) Moderately
( ) Most of the time
( ) Very

18. Even when I'm sitting (a) silently, I usually keep moving my hands or feet.

( ) Never
( ) Just a little
( ) Reasonably
( ) Moderately
( ) Most of the time
( ) Very

19. In group activities, it is very difficult to have to wait my turn.

( ) Never

( ) Just a little
( ) Reasonably
( ) Moderately
( ) Most of the time
( ) Very

20. My mind is always so confused that it seems difficult to achieve a good mental functioning.

( ) Never
( ) Just a little
( ) Reasonably
( ) Moderately
( ) Most of the time
( ) Very

21. I think of several things simultaneously, and my thoughts seem to move as if my mind were an arcade machine.

( ) Never
( ) Just a little
( ) Reasonably
( ) Moderately
( ) Most of the time
( ) Very

22. My brain looks like a television set with all channels connected at the same time.

( ) Never
( ) Just a little
( ) Reasonably
( ) Moderately
( ) Most of the time
( ) Very

23. When I'm daydreaming it's even hard to stop "daydreaming."

( ) Never
( ) Just a little
( ) Reasonably
( ) Moderately
( ) Most of the time
( ) Very

24. I am distressed by the disorganized way of functioning my brain.

( ) Never
( ) Just a little
( ) Reasonably
( ) Moderately
( ) Most of the time
( ) Very

How to Evaluate

From 0 to 24 points — Probably has no **ADHD**

From 25 to 34 points — Has only a few symptoms of **ADHD**

From 35 to 49 points — The evaluated person probably has **ADHD** with average current severity.

From 50 to 69 points — The evaluated person probably has **ADHD** with moderate current severity.

Above 70 points — The evaluated person has **ADHD**

NOTE*: it should be taken into account even that, high scores in this exam can result from episodes of anxiety, depression or mania. These conditions should be discarded before a diagnosis of **ADHD** in adults can be confirmed.

Conners Evaluation Scales
–Versions for Parents and Teachers –

Among the most commonly used instruments today to verify the diagnostic characteristics of Attention Deficit Hyperactivity Disorder **(ADHD)** highlighted by conners rating scales, Conners Evaluation Scales — Versions for Parents and Teachers. Prepared in 1969 by the then American psychologist, Carmen Keith Conners, the scale was slightly adapted to other countries, and with its wide diffusion became one of the best evaluated tools to verify the presence of **ADHD** symptoms. However, despite all its efficacy recognized worldwide, because it presents a structure similar to that of a semi-structured interview, its application alone, cannot ratify the diagnosis of **ADHD.**

Conners Scale for Teachers - Reduced Version

Below are the most frequent problems that affect children during their developmental process. And while many of these characteristics are appropriate for normal behaviors, it should be carefully examined whether these manifestations have high levels of intensity, frequency and / or duration. Thus, the questions below should be answered considering the child's behavior during the last month. Therefore, it is recommended that, for each item, ask yourself, "How often has this happened in the last month?" Then, for each of the 28 propositions presented, mark 1 of the 4 answers below that best corresponds to the person evaluated.

1. **Never = 0 Points**
2. **A Little = 1 Point**
3. **Often = 2 Points**
4. **Very Often = 3 Points**

1. Inattentive (a). Easily get distracted

( ) Never
( ) A Little
( ) Often
( ) Very Often

2. Challenging behavior with adults

( ) Never
( ) A Little
( ) Often
( ) Very Often

3. Restless (a). It seems to have "carpenter animals" (stir so the body without leaving place)

( ) Never
( ) A Little
( ) Often
( ) Very Often

4. Forget things he (a) had already learned

( ) Never
( ) A Little
( ) Often
( ) Very Often

5. Disturbs other children

( ) Never
( ) A Little
( ) Often
( ) Very Often

6. Challenges the adult and does not collaborate with the requests made to him

( ) Never
( ) A Little
( ) Often
( ) Very Often

7. Move a lot as it is always "connected (a) to an engine"

( ) Never
( ) A Little
( ) Often
( ) Very Often

8. Spells poorly

( ) Never
( ) A Little
( ) Often
( ) Very Often

9. Can't stay quiet (a) for long

( ) Never
( ) A Little
( ) Often
( ) Very Often

10. Vengeful (a) or evil (a)

( ) Never
( ) A Little
( ) Often
( ) Very Often

11. You get up from the place in the classroom or in other situations where you should sit (a)

( ) Never
( ) A Little
( ) Often
( ) Very Often

12. Move your feet and/or hands and are restless (a) in your place

( ) Never
( ) A Little
( ) Often
( ) Very Often

13. Read capacity below expected

( ) Never
( ) A Little

( ) Often
( ) Very Often

14. Have a short time of attention

( ) Never
( ) A Little
( ) Often
( ) Very Often

15. Usually argue or challenge adults

( ) Never
( ) A Little
( ) Often
( ) Very Often

16. Directs attention only to matters that interest you

( ) Never
( ) A Little
( ) Often
( ) Very Often

17. Have difficulty waiting your turn

( ) Never
( ) A Little
( ) Often
( ) Very Often

18. Demonstrates disinterest in schoolwork

( ) Never
( ) A Little

( ) Often
( ) Very Often

19. Distracted (a) or presenting short attention time

( ) Never
( ) A Little
( ) Often
( ) Very Often

20. Has an explosive and unpredictable temperament

( ) Never
( ) A Little
( ) Often
( ) Very Often

21. Runs around space or over-galga in situations where such behaviors are inappropriate

( ) Never
( ) A Little
( ) Often
( ) Very Often

22. Poor in arithmetic

( ) Never
( ) A Little
( ) Often
( ) Very Often

23. Interrupt and/or intrude in the games or conversations of other

( ) Never
( ) A Little
( ) Often
( ) Very Often

24. Have difficulty engaging in games or leisure activities, in a quiet way

( ) Never
( ) A Little
( ) Often
( ) Very Often

25. Generally, it does not complete the things that begins

( ) Never
( ) A Little
( ) Often
( ) Very Often

26. It does not usually follow the instructions given to it and does not complete school activities (not due to opposition behaviors, nor because of a lack of understanding of what has been asked of)

( ) Never
( ) A Little
( ) Often
( ) Very Often

27. Excitable and impulsive (a)

( ) Never

( ) A Little
( ) Often
( ) Very Often

28. Restless (a). He's always getting up from the chair and moving around the room space.

( ) Never
( ) A Little
( ) Often
( ) Very Often

Conners Scale for Parents - Reduced Version

The following will be presented the most frequent problems affecting children during their development process. And, although many Dess the characteristics are appropriate to normal behaviors, it should be carefully analyzed if these manifestations present high values in intensity, frequency and/or duration levels. Thus, the questions below should be answered considering the behavior of the child during the last month. Therefore, it is recommended that, for each item, ask yourself, "How often has this occurred in the last month?" Then, for each of the 27 propositions presented, Marquand 1 of the 4 answers below that best corresponds to the evaluated person.

1. **Never = 0 Points**
2. **A Little = 1 Point**
3. **Often = 2 Points**
4. **Very Often = 3 Points**

1. Inattentive. Easily get distracted.

( ) Never
( ) A Little
( ) Often
( ) Very Often

2. Furious. It gets angry with ease and is resentful.

( ) Never

( ) A Little
( ) Often
( ) Very Often

3.Difficulty in doing or finishing homework

( ) Never
( ) A Little
( ) Often
( ) Very Often

4.You are always moving or acting as "having batteries charged" or as if "connected to an engine"

( ) Never
( ) A Little
( ) Often
( ) Very Often

5.Short attention time

( ) Never
( ) A Little
( ) Often
( ) Very Often

6.Discusses and/or argues with adults in an inappropriate manner

( ) Never
( ) A Little
( ) Often
( ) Very Often

7.Stir your feet and hands a lot and move even if you sit in place

( ) Never
( ) A Little
( ) Often
( ) Very Often

8.Generally, you can't and/or have difficulty completing your activities

( ) Never
( ) A Little
( ) Often
( ) Very Often

9.   Difficult to control in shopping centers or public places

( ) Never
( ) A Little
( ) Often
( ) Very Often

10.Messy and/or disorganized at home and/or school

( ) Never
( ) A Little
( ) Often
( ) Very Often

11. Irascible. Loses control with ease

( ) Never
( ) A Little

( ) Often
( ) Very Often

12.Need to be charged or accompanied to perform your tasks

( ) Never
( ) A Little
( ) Often
( ) Very Often

13.Only pay attention to things that interest you

( ) Never
( ) A Little
( ) Often
( ) Very Often

14.Runs around space or over-galga in situations where such behaviors are inappropriate

( ) Never
( ) A Little
( ) Often
( ) Very Often

15.Distracted (a) and/or with a short attention time

( ) Never
( ) A Little
( ) Often
( ) Very Often

16.Irritable

( ) Never
( ) A Little
( ) Often
( ) Very Often

17.Avoids, expresses reluctance or has difficulty in undertaking tasks that require continued mental effort (such as school or homework)

( ) Never
( ) A Little
( ) Often
( ) Very Often

18.Restless(a) it seems that "has carpenter sbugs" (stirs the body without leaving place)

( ) Never
( ) A Little
( ) Often
( ) Very Often

19.Get distracted when they're giving you instructions to do something

( ) Never
( ) A Little
( ) Often
( ) Very Often

20.Challenges the adult or refuses to satisfy the requests made to him

( ) Never
( ) A Little
( ) Often
( ) Very Often

21. Demonstrates concentration problems during classes

( ) Never
( ) A Little
( ) Often
( ) Very Often

22.Have difficulty staying in a queue or waiting for your turn in a game or group work

( ) Never
( ) A Little
( ) Often
( ) Very Often

23.Get up in the room or in places where you should sit

( ) Never
( ) A Little
( ) Often
( ) Very Often

24.Deliberately does things to annoy others

( ) Never
( ) A Little
( ) Often
( ) Very Often

25.Does not follow instructions and normally, does not terminate work, tasks and obligations in place (it is not difficult to understand instructions or refusal)

( ) Never
( ) A Little
( ) Often
( ) Very Often

26.Have difficulty playing or working quietly

( ) Never
( ) A Little
( ) Often
( ) Very Often

27.Get frustrated when you can't do anything

( ) Never
( ) A Little
( ) Often
( ) Very Often

Conners Scale for Parents and Teachers
Version adapted and validated for use in Brazil

Adapted and validated in Brazil by Barbosa in 1995, the integrated version of the Conners scale for parents and teachers consists of four factors distributed among 81 propositions, which are characterized by the resulting profile of children and/or adolescents with **ADHD.** Thus, while some scales investigate only the presence of current symptomatic manifestations, the Conners Evaluation Scales also allow, to analyze systematically, each of the symptoms contemplated by **DSM,** dating back to childhood and adolescence.

1. **Never = 0 Points**
2. **Sometimes = 1 Point**
3. **Often = 2 Points**
4. **Always = 3 Points**

Parent version - Cutoff point equal to 58

1. Usual behavior at home

Wakes up at night

( ) Never
( ) Sometimes
( ) Often
( ) Always

You're afraid in the face of new situations

( ) Never
( ) Sometimes
( ) Often
( ) Always

You're afraid of people

( ) Never
( ) Sometimes
( ) Often
( ) Always

You're afraid you're alone

( ) Never
( ) Sometimes
( ) Often
( ) Always

He cares about diseases and deaths

( ) Never
( ) Sometimes
( ) Often
( ) Always

It is tense and rigid

( ) Never
( ) Sometimes
( ) Often
( ) Always

Presents muscle spasms

( ) Never
( ) Sometimes
( ) Often
( ) Always

It presents tremors

( ) Never
( ) Sometimes
( ) Often
( ) Always

You feel headaches

( ) Never
( ) Sometimes
( ) Often
( ) Always

You feel stomach pains

( ) Never
( ) Sometimes
( ) Often
( ) Always

There's vomiting

( ) Never
( ) Sometimes
( ) Often
( ) Always

Complains of illnesses and pains

( ) Never

( ) Sometimes
( ) Often
( ) Always

Let yourself be carried away by other children

( ) Never
( ) Sometimes
( ) Often
( ) Always

Challenges and intimidates others

( ) Never
( ) Sometimes
( ) Often
( ) Always

He is brave (arrogant) and disrespects his superiors (insolent)

( ) Never
( ) Sometimes
( ) Often
( ) Always

It is brazen with adults

( ) Never
( ) Sometimes
( ) Often
( ) Always

He's shy in front of his friends

( ) Never
( ) Sometimes

( ) Often
( ) Always

Fear not to please your friends

( ) Never
( ) Sometimes
( ) Often
( ) Always

Have friends

( ) Never
( ) Sometimes
( ) Often
( ) Always

It's malicious with your brothers

( ) Never
( ) Sometimes
( ) Often
( ) Always

Fight constantly

( ) Never
( ) Sometimes
( ) Often
( ) Always

Criticizes many other children

( ) Never
( ) Sometimes
( ) Often

( ) Always

Learn in school

( ) Never
( ) Sometimes
( ) Often
( ) Always

Likes to go to school

( ) Never
( ) Sometimes
( ) Often
( ) Always

You're afraid to go to school

( ) Never
( ) Sometimes
( ) Often
( ) Always

Disobeys school standards

( ) Never
( ) Sometimes
( ) Often
( ) Always

Mind, blaming others for their mistakes

( ) Never
( ) Sometimes
( ) Often
( ) Always

Steals from your parents

( ) Never
( ) Sometimes
( ) Often
( ) Always

Performs thefts at school

( ) Never
( ) Sometimes
( ) Often
( ) Always

Steals in shops, tents and elsewhere

( ) Never
( ) Sometimes
( ) Often
( ) Always

You have problems with the police.

( ) Never
( ) Sometimes
( ) Often
( ) Always

You want to do everything well done (perfectionist)

( ) Never
( ) Sometimes
( ) Often
( ) Always

You always need to do things the same way

( ) Never
( ) Sometimes
( ) Often
( ) Always

It has great goals (dreams loudly)

( ) Never
( ) Sometimes
( ) Often
( ) Always

Easily get distracted

( ) Never
( ) Sometimes
( ) Often
( ) Always

It is nervous and restless

( ) Never
( ) Sometimes
( ) Often
( ) Always

Can't be quiet

( ) Never
( ) Sometimes
( ) Often
( ) Always

Rises everywhere

( ) Never

( ) Sometimes
( ) Often
( ) Always

Wakes up too early

( ) Never
( ) Sometimes
( ) Often
( ) Always

Don't be quiet during meals

( ) Never
( ) Sometimes
( ) Often
( ) Always

If you start doing something repetitive, you have difficulty stopping

( ) Never
( ) Sometimes
( ) Often
( ) Always

Their attitudes appear to be driven by an engine

( ) Never
( ) Sometimes
( ) Often
( ) Always

Teacher version - Cutoff point equal to 62

2. Classroom behavior

It's constantly moving

( ) Never
( ) Sometimes
( ) Often
( ) Always

Emits sounds, noises

( ) Never
( ) Sometimes
( ) Often
( ) Always

He likes that your orders will be slightly fulfilled

( ) Never
( ) Sometimes
( ) Often
( ) Always

Has compromised motor coordination

( ) Never
( ) Sometimes
( ) Often
( ) Always

Restless, superactive

( ) Never
( ) Sometimes
( ) Often
( ) Always

Excitable, impulsive

( ) Never
( ) Sometimes
( ) Often
( ) Always

Inattentive and easily distracted

( ) Never
( ) Sometimes
( ) Often
( ) Always

Normally, it does not end what begins

( ) Never
( ) Sometimes
( ) Often
( ) Always

Overly sensitive

( ) Never
( ) Sometimes
( ) Often
( ) Always

Extremely serious and/or sad

( ) Never
( ) Sometimes
( ) Often
( ) Always

Dream awakes

( ) Never
( ) Sometimes
( ) Often
( ) Always

Grumpy, grumpy

( ) Never
( ) Sometimes
( ) Often
( ) Always

Cry with ease

( ) Never
( ) Sometimes
( ) Often
( ) Always

Disturbs other children

( ) Never
( ) Sometimes
( ) Often
( ) Always

Causes confusion

( ) Never
( ) Sometimes
( ) Often
( ) Always

Mood oscillates dramatically and quickly

( ) Never

( ) Sometimes
( ) Often
( ) Always

Cunning, he likes to play the smart guy

( ) Never
( ) Sometimes
( ) Often
( ) Always

Destructive

( ) Never
( ) Sometimes
( ) Often
( ) Always

Iridescent

( ) Never
( ) Sometimes
( ) Often
( ) Always

Mind

( ) Never
( ) Sometimes
( ) Often
( ) Always

Bursts of anger, unpredictable, explosive behavior

( ) Never
( ) Sometimes

( ) Often
( ) Always

3. Group Participation

Isolates from other children

( ) Never
( ) Sometimes
( ) Often
( ) Always

It doesn't seem to be accepted by the group

( ) Never
( ) Sometimes
( ) Often
( ) Always

It seems to get carried away easily

( ) Never
( ) Sometimes
( ) Often
( ) Always

Does not demonstrate "sportsmanship"

( ) Never
( ) Sometimes
( ) Often
( ) Always

You don't seem to have leadership skills

( ) Never

( ) Sometimes
( ) Often
( ) Always

It doesn't relate well to the opposite sex

( ) Never
( ) Sometimes
( ) Often
( ) Always

It doesn't relate well to same-sex children

( ) Never
( ) Sometimes
( ) Often
( ) Always

It causes other children or interferes with their activities deliberately

( ) Never
( ) Sometimes
( ) Often
( ) Always

4. Attitude towards authorities

Submissive

( ) Never
( ) Sometimes
( ) Often
( ) Always

Challenging

( ) Never
( ) Sometimes
( ) Often
( ) Always

Sassy

( ) Never
( ) Sometimes
( ) Often
( ) Always

Shy

( ) Never
( ) Sometimes
( ) Often
( ) Always

Scared

( ) Never
( ) Sometimes
( ) Often
( ) Always

Excessive attention requirement. Mainly, from the teacher

( ) Never
( ) Sometimes
( ) Often
( ) Always

Stubborn

( ) Never

( ) Sometimes
( ) Often
( ) Always

Overly eager to please

( ) Never
( ) Sometimes
( ) Often
( ) Always

Non-cooperation

( ) Never
( ) Sometimes
( ) Often
( ) Always

Lack of classes often

( ) Never
( ) Sometimes
( ) Often
( ) Always

Structured Adults ADHD Self-Test (SAAST)

Developed by Dr. Greg Mulhauser, Structured Self-testing for adults with **ADHD** is a screening assessment that serves only as an indicative resource for the diagnosis of **ADHD** in adults. Formed by 22 questions that differ between two distinct components of the diagnosis of **ADHD** (inattention along with hyperactivity/impulsivity) this tool is also sensitive to factors that normally prevent the diagnosis of **ADHD.**

How to Use

According to the values presented for the 4 response options, the 22 sentences proposed below should correspond to the way the person evaluated felt and behaved during most of their adult life.

1. **No, no way = 0 Points**
2. **Yes, a little = 1 Point**
3. **Yes, moderately = 2 Points**
4. **Yes, very = 3 Points**

1. I found that I made mistakes at work, at school, or in other activities because I have difficulty paying attention to the details.

( ) No, no way

( ) Yes, a little

( ) Yes, moderately

( ) Yes, very

2. I tend to mess with my hands, feet, or squirm, often, in places that should remain quiet.

( ) No, no way

( ) Yes, a little

( ) Yes, moderately

( ) Yes, very

3. I often get distracted and lose myself in what's being said in conversations.

( ) No, no way

( ) Yes, a little

( ) Yes, moderately

( ) Yes, very

4. I prefer to run or climb things, even when I know it doesn't fit the situation.

( ) No, no way

( ) Yes, a little

( ) Yes, moderately

( ) Yes, very

5. I find it difficult to organize my tasks and/or activities.

( ) No, no way

( ) Yes, a little

( ) Yes, moderately

( ) Yes, very

6. I'm often "on the go."

( ) No, no way

( ) Yes, a little

( ) Yes, moderately

( ) Yes, very

7. I usually lose things I need to use not school or not work.

( ) No, no way

( ) Yes, a little

( ) Yes, moderately

( ) Yes, very

8. I can't help but answer before someone's even done asking me a question.

( ) No, no way

( ) Yes, a little

( ) Yes, moderately

( ) Yes, very

9. I am forgotten during my daily activities.

( ) No, no way

( ) Yes, a little

( ) Yes, moderately

( ) Yes, very

10. I find it difficult to keep my attention on what I'm doing, whether it's working or playing.

( ) No, no way

( ) Yes, a little

( ) Yes, moderately

( ) Yes, very

11. I find it hard to sit, even when I know I need to wait for something.

( ) No, no way

( ) Yes, a little

( ) Yes, moderately

( ) Yes, very

12. I find it difficult to follow instructions or complete tasks or duties, even understanding that is what is expected of me.

( ) No, no way

( ) Yes, a little

( ) Yes, moderately

( ) Yes, very

13. I find it difficult to engage in playful activities athleisure u that are silent.

( ) No, no way

( ) Yes, a little

( ) Yes, moderately

( ) Yes, very

14. I don't like having to do something that requires sustained mental effort.

( ) No, no way

( ) Yes, a little

( ) Yes, moderately

( ) Yes, very

15. I usually talk excessively.

( ) No, no way

( ) Yes, a little

( ) Yes, moderately

( ) Yes, very

16. I'm easily distracted.

( ) No, no way

( ) Yes, a little

( ) Yes, moderately

( ) Yes, very

17. I have trouble waiting my turn.

( ) No, no way

( ) Yes, a little

( ) Yes, moderately

( ) Yes, very

18. I often interrupt others.

( ) No, no way

( ) Yes, a little

( ) Yes, moderately

( ) Yes, very

19. Even before the age of 7, some of the previous questions (1-18) would still have been marked "Yes, moderately" or "Yes, too".

( ) No

( ) Yes

20. I have problems related to some of the above situations in more than one context. That is, I have manifestations of these problems not only at home, nor only at work.

( ) No

( ) Yes

21. The presence of these problems usually triggers some harm and social, academic, professional and/or my interpersonal relationships.

( ) No, no way

( ) Yes, a little

( ) Yes, moderately

( ) Yes, very

22. I have been diagnosed before with another **Disorder which could also justify** the types **of experiences proposed above. Or I believe you might be going through such a mess. This may include Invasive Developmental Disorder, Mood Disorder, Anxiety Disorder, Dissociative Disorder, Personality Disorder, Schizophrenia or other Psychotic Disorder.**

( ) No

( ) Yes

How to Evaluate

Score for questions 1-18:

0 — No, no way
1 — Yes, a little
2 — Yes, moderately
3 — Yes, very

This produces a total maximum score of 54. Question 21 is scored on the same scale; however, it is used to judge whether an **ADHD** diagnosis should be excluded. Therefore, it should not be included in the final total of the points. Questions 19, 20 and 22 with the possibility of answers only to YES / NO scored as a binary choice and are used again to rule out the diagnosis of **ADHD**. For example, question 19 about the presence of symptoms before age 7.

Additional Information

Scores above 24, along with the absence of mitigating factors (other medical conditions) are generally consistent for the presence of **ADHD.** Therefore, if the evaluated person obtained more than 24 points in this test it is recommended that him seek an expert to perform a more detailed and accurate evaluation.

Initial Questionnaire for Parents and Teachers

Composed of 120 sentences, the integrated version of the Initial Questionnaire for Parents (QIPAIS) and the Initial Questionnaire for Teachers (QIPROF) was developed by joining the characteristics present in 4 different tools used in the diagnosis of **ADHD**: **(1)** DSM, **(2)** Child Behavior Checklist (CBCL), **(3)** and Scala de Conners, **(4)** SNAP-IV.

How to Use

Following will be related to the descriptive terms of behavior of your student (a) or child(a). Read, carefully, each item, and according to the 5 abbreviated response options below, check the one that best matches the evaluated person.

1. **Never / Not A Little = (NL)**
2. **Sometimes / Rarely = (SR)**
3. **Oftentimes / Frequently = (OF)**
4. **Always = (A)**
5. **Don't Know Inform= (DKI)**

1. Failure to pay attention to detail or make mistakes for lack of care in schoolwork and tasks

(N L)

(S R)

(O F)

(A)

(D K I)

2. Difficulty finishing what begins

(N L)

(S R)

(O F)

(A)

(D K I)

3. It is disorganized in your class lessons, tasks or activities

(N L)

(S R)

(O F)

(A)

(D K I)

4. Forget daily activities (tasks, errands, obligations)

(N L)

(S R)

(O F)

(A)

(D K I)

5. Doesn't seem to hear when they talk to him

(N L)

(S R)

(O F)

(A)

(D K I)

6. Unable to pay attention to the same thing for a long time

(N L)

(S R)

(O F)

(A)

(D K I)

7. Have difficulties to follow instructions, terminate homework, tasks, or obligations

(N L)

(S R)

(O F)

(A)

(D K I)

8. Easily distracted by noises or other stimuli in class

(N L)

(S R)

(O F)

(A)

(DKI)

9. Avoids, dislikes or refutes in participating in tasks and games that require mental effort

(NL)

(SR)

(OF)

(A)

(DKI)

10. Loses things (toys, books, pencils, notebooks, jackets, slippers)

(NL)

(SR)

(OF)

(A)

(DKI)

11. Has difficulty staying tuned during explanations, to respond to requests or execute orders

(NL)

(SR)

(OF)

(A)

(D K I)

12. Have difficulty keeping an eye on tasks or games

(N L)

(S R)

(O F)

(A)

(D K I)

13. Lives dreaming, in the "world of the moon"

(N L)

(S R)

(O F)

(A)

(D K I)

14. Difficulty in paying attention to an activity or conversation

(N L)

(S R)

(O F)

(A)

(D K I)

15. Quickly forget what has just been said

(N L)

(S R)

(O F)

(A)

(D K I)

16. School activities are usually delayed

(N L)

(S R)

(O F)

(A)

(D K I)

17. Difficulty in fulfilling orders

(N L)

(S R)

(O F)

(A)

(D K I)

18. Difficulty following instructions

(N L)

(S R)

(O F)

(A)

(D K I)

19. Difficulty to wait the turn

(N L)

(S R)

(O F)

(A)

(D K I)

20. Age recklessly (risks)

(N L)

(S R)

(O F)

(A)

(D K I)

21. Do tasks quickly to feel livre.

(N L)

(S R)

(O F)

(A)

(D K I)

22. Answer before hearing any question

(N L)

(S R)

(O F)

(A)

(D K I)

23. It always appears to be "at full steam" or "connected in an engine"

(N L)

(S R)

(O F)

(A)

(D K I)

24. Acts without thinking (it's impulsive)

(N L)

(S R)

(O F)

(A)

(D K I)

25. Interrupt or intrude in conversations, pranks

(N L)

(S R)

(O F)

(A)

(D K I)

26. Too much speech (hinders class)

(N L)

(S R)

(O F)

(A)

(D K I)

27. Have difficulty to stay sitting. If it stirs and/or rises from the chairs

(N L)

(S R)

(O F)

(A)

(D K I)

28. Have difficulty playing or silently participating in leisure activities

(N L)

(S R)

(O F)

(A)

(D K I)

29. Too much conversation (disrupts the environment or class)

(N L)

(S R)

(O F)

(A)

(D K I)

30. Runs or climbs through the walls in inappropriate situations

(N L)

(S R)

(O F)

(A)

(D K I)

31. It is impatient and restless

(N L)

(S R)

(O F)

(A)

(D K I)

32. Requires your requests to be met immediately

(N L)

(S R)

(O F)

(A)

(D K I)

33. Shakes hands and feet and shakes in chair/wallet

(N L)

(S R)

(O F)

(A)

(D K I)

34. Breaks or destroys school material or other objects

(N L)

(S R)

(O F)

(A)

(D K I)

35. Suffers Accidents Easily

(N L)

(S R)

(O F)

(A)

(D K I)

36. Speaks with difficulty

(N L)

(S R)

(O F)

(A)

(D K I)

37. Difficulty in drafting texts (summarizing, lack of content or coherence)

(N L)

(S R)

(O F)

(A)

(D K I)

38. Slow reading, silachia, faltering, non-automated

(N L)

(S R)

(O F)

(A)

(D K I)

39. Difficulty in interpreting texts read

(N L)

(S R)

(O F)

(A)

(D K I)

40. Difficulty in interpreting written texts

(N L)

(S R)

(O F)

(A)

(D K I)

41. Presents difficulties in writing: exchanges, substitutions, mirroring or agglutination

(N L)

(S R)

(O F)

(A)

(D K I)

42. Presents sloppy calligraphy

(N L)

(S R)

(O F)

(A)

(D K I)

43. Presents inadequate accentuation and scores

(N L)

(S R)

(O F)

(A)

(D K I)

44. Logical reasoning is slow

(N L)

(S R)

(O F)

(A)

(D K I)

45. Failure to solve mathematical problems

(N L)

(S R)

(O F)

(A)

(D K I)

46. Performs mathematical operations with difficulty (according to series)

(N L)

(S R)

(O F)

(A)

(D K I)

47. Yields below expected at school

(N L)

(S R)

(O F)

(A)

(D K I)

48. Have difficulty expressing your thoughts orally

(N L)

(S R)

(O F)

(A)

(D K I)

49. Avoids tasks that require constant mental effort

(N L)

(S R)

(O F)

(A)

(D K I)

50. Presents difficulty in fine motricity (drawings, lace, tie, button, use scissors)

(NL)

(SR)

(OF)

(A)

(DKI)

51. Presents difficulty in global motricity (balance, falls frequently)

(NL)

(SR)

(OF)

(A)

(DKI)

52. Avoids school tasks or work

(NL)

(SR)

(OF)

(A)

(DKI)

53. Avoids studying (lack of motivation to study and do tasks)

(NL)

(SR)

(OF)

(A)

(D K I)

54. Participates little in class and asks for help when necessary

(N L)

(S R)

(O F)

(A)

(D K I)

55. Studies little for evaluations

(N L)

(S R)

(O F)

(A)

(D K I)

56. Loses calm easily (short wick)

(N L)

(S R)

(O F)

(A)

(D K I)

57. Discusses with adults (cheeky, debauched, bold)

(N L)

(S R)

(O F)

(A)

(D K I)

58. It is bully or aggressive with other people

(N L)

(S R)

(O F)

(A)

(D K I)

59. Challenges or refuses to follow the rules or requests/requests such as brushing your teeth, bathing, doing chores

(N L)

(S R)

(O F)

(A)

(D K I)

60. Does purpose-based things that bother or interfere with the activities

(N L)

(S R)

(O F)

(A)

(D K I)

61. Blames others for their errors or misconduct

(N L)

(S R)

(O F)

(A)

(D K I)

62. Disturbs other children (irritates other children with antics, jerks or pokes)

(N L)

(S R)

(O F)

(A)

(D K I)

63. It is brave and/or resentful

(N L)

(S R)

(O F)

(A)

(D K I)

64. Hate guard or is vengeful

(N L)
(S R)
(O F)
(A)
(D K I)

65. Is a negativist, defiant, disobedient or hostile against

(N L)
(S R)
(O F)
(A)
(D K I)

66. Hurts other children

(N L)
(S R)
(O F)
(A)
(D K I)

67. Steal something (money, school supplies, toys)

(N L)

(S R)

(O F)

(A)

(D K I)

68. Easily frustrated if not met

(N L)

(S R)

(O F)

(A)

(D K I)

69. It's grumpy

(N L)

(S R)

(O F)

(A)

(D K I)

70. Destroys the property of the other people (vandalism)

(N L)

(S R)

(O F)

(A)

(D K I)

71. He is a liar (mind, fraud, glue, copies work, cheats)

(NL)

(SR)

(OF)

(A)

(DKI)

72. Violates the rules seriously - gauze class, flees, ignores class rules

(NL)

(SR)

(OF)

(A)

(DKI)

73. Cooperates little with teachers and/or colleagues

(NL)

(SR)

(OF)

(A)

(DKI)

74. Acts smartly (rascal), always wants to take advantage

(NL)

(SR)

(OF)

(A)

(DKI)

75. Is manipulator

(NL)

(SR)

(OF)

(A)

(DKI)

76. Presents access of fury / has explosive temperament

(NL)

(SR)

(OF)

(A)

(DKI)

77. It is rejected by colleagues or family members

(NL)

(SR)

(OF)

(A)

(DKI)

78. Difficulties in accepting limits

(NL)

(SR)

(OF)

(A)

(DKI)

79. Causes confusion in meetings, parties, parks or classroom

(NL)

(SR)

(OF)

(A)

(DKI)

80. It's sad, empty or unhappy

(NL)

(SR)

(OF)

(A)

(DKI)

81. Cries Easy

(NL)

(SR)

(OF)

(A)

(D K I)

82. Feels guilty or useless or incapable or finds it ugly

(N L)

(S R)

(O F)

(A)

(D K I)

83. Lack of interest or pleasure in activities (discouragement or tasteless for things or indisposition)

(N L)

(S R)

(O F)

(A)

(D K I)

84. Get tired

(N L)

(S R)

(O F)

(A)

(D K I)

85. Presents exaggerated lack or appetite

(NL)

(SR)

(OF)

(A)

(DKI)

86. Isolates or plays only

(NL)

(SR)

(OF)

(A)

(DKI)

87. Talks about dying or having ideas, plans or suicide attempt

(NL)

(SR)

(OF)

(A)

(DKI)

88. Persistent physical symptoms - headache, or abdominal or legs, diarrhea, vomiting, dizziness

(NL)

(SR)

(OF)

(A)

(D K I)

89. Have anxiety or excessive concern

(N L)

(S R)

(O F)

(A)

(D K I)

90. Presents low self-esteem most of the time

(N L)

(S R)

(O F)

(A)

(D K I)

91. Inconsequential in their acts (it does not care about the opinion of others)

(N L)

(S R)

(O F)

(A)

(D K I)

92. It is pessimistic, discouraged or hopeless

(N L)

(S R)

(O F)

(A)

(D K I)

93. Variable mood (sadness and/or irritability)

(N L)

(S R)

(O F)

(A)

(D K I)

94. Has fears or crises of panic

(N L)

(S R)

(O F)

(A)

(D K I)

95. It has compulsions (repetitive behaviors or acts to reduce anxiety or anguish: cleaning mania, checking if the door is open, repetition how to count numbers etc.)

(N L)

(S R)

(O F)

(A)

(D K I)

96. Has manias or rituals

(N L)

(S R)

(O F)

(A)

(D K I)

97. Speaks or makes intentional obscene gestures

(N L)

(S R)

(O F)

(A)

(D K I)

98. Makes strange noises (sniffle, strange sounds, profanity)

(N L)

(S R)

(O F)

(A)

(D K I)

99. It has some nerve tic (blinks, stirs with hands, shoulders,

arms, nail roi, sucks fingers)

(N L)

(S R)

(O F)

(A)

(D K I)

100. Worries about illness or death

(N L)

(S R)

(O F)

(A)

(D K I)

101. Presents euphoria, exaggerated or inappropriate joy

(N L)

(S R)

(O F)

(A)

(D K I)

102. Ideas of greatness, thinks "the best"

(N L)

(S R)

(O F)

(A)

(D K I)

103. Brave - faces situations inconsequentially

(N L)

(S R)

(O F)

(A)

(D K I)

104. Inappropriate sexual behavior (force sexual act, abuse, misconduct)

(N L)

(S R)

(O F)

(A)

(D K I)

105. Avoids looking into the eyes of others

(N L)

(S R)

(O F)

(A)

(D K I)

106. Presents abnormal movements (jumps, claps, shakes

hands, touches people)

(N L)

(S R)

(O F)

(A)

(D K I)

107. It's selfish

(N L)

(S R)

(O F)

(A)

(D K I)

108. Acts incorrectly: eliminates gases, spit, pushes others

(N L)

(S R)

(O F)

(A)

(D K I)

109. Difficulty memorizing

(N L)

(S R)

(O F)

(A)

(DKI)

110. Injures and harms animals (cruel)

(NL)

(SR)

(OF)

(A)

(DKI)

111. Starts fights or physical struggles

(NL)

(SR)

(OF)

(A)

(DKI)

112. Usually intimidates or threatens others

(NL)

(SR)

(OF)

(A)

(DKI)

113. Usually leaves urine or feces in clothes

(N L)

(S R)

(O F)

(A)

(D K I)

114.   Constantly   varies   from   behavior (sadness/euphoria/agitation)

(N L)

(S R)

(O F)

(A)

(D K I)

115. Concerns about the future (with things before it happens)

(N L)

(S R)

(O F)

(A)

(D K I)

116. It is undecided

(N L)

(S R)

(O F)

(A)

(DKI)

117. Concerns about past facts

(NL)

(SR)

(OF)

(A)

(DKI)

118. He's usually angry

(NL)

(SR)

(OF)

(A)

(DKI)

119. Presents obsessive, unpleasant, uncomfortable thoughts

(NL)

(SR)

(OF)

(A)

(DKI)

120. Presents sleep problems (insomnia, nightmares, sleepwalking, sleeping talk)

(N L)

(S R)

(O F)

(A)

(D K I)

Considerations

1. The difficulties presented above interfere and/or hinder his learning:

No ( )

Yes ( )

Do not know ( )

2. The difficulties presented above interfere and/or hinder his relationship with other children, teachers, school staff and/or family members:

No ( )

Yes ( )

Do not know ( )

Wender Utah Assessment Scale for ADHD

Consisting of 61 items and a subset with 25 questions associated with the diagnosis of **ADHD,** the Wender Utah Rating Scale (WURS), Wender Utah Evaluation Scale is a self-report instrument designed for retrospective dimensional evaluation of **ADHD** in childhood for adults and has been widely used in this context. According to the latest research it has also been found that the scale can be used appropriately to predict cases of dysthymia, oppositional defiant disorder, schoolwork problems, conduct disorder, and anxiety disorders in adults with ADHD. Based on the DSM criteria, the Wender Utah Rating Scale measures adult ADHD symptoms through seven categories:

1. Attention Difficulties;
2. Hyperactivity/Restlessness;
3. Temperament;
4. Affective Lability;
5. Emotional Hyper-Reactivity;
6. Disorganization;
7. Impulsivity;

How to Use

The 61 sentences should be answered by the adult evaluated, considering their behaviors during childhood (As a child, I was or had...). And from its conclusions, point out the value for response options that best represents the condition of the evaluated person.

1. **Not a little or too slightly = 0 Points**
2. **Smoothly = 1 Point**
3. **Moderately = 2 Points**
4. **Quite = 3 Points**
5. **Very = 4 Points**

As a child, I was (or had)

1.Active, agitated and was always on the move

2.I was afraid of many things

3.Concentration problems, easily distracted

4.Worry, anxiety

5.Nervous, restless

6.Unattentive, "dreamed awake"

7.Boiling point, "low or high" temperature

8.Sensitive shy

9.Explosive temperament, anger accesses

10.Difficulty with persistence to finish the things that began

11.Stubborn, obstinate

12.Sad, unhappy or depressed

13.Incauta and/or diabolical in the games

14.Didn't enjoy things, dissatisfied with life

15.Rebellious, disobedient and sassy with my parents

16.Low opinion about myself

17.Irritable

18.Extroverted and friendly in the company of persons

19.Sloppy, disorganized

20.High and low mood

21.Brava

22.Popular friends

23.Well organized, tidy

24.Acting impulsively, without thinking

25.Tendency to be immature

26. Feelings of guilt, of repentant

27.Lost control of myself

28.Tendency to be or act irrationally

29.Unpopular with other children, I didn't keep friends for long, I didn't relate well to other children

30. Uncoordinated, did not participate in sports

31.Fear of losing control

32.Had good motor coordination, was the first choice in games

33.Brazen (women only)

34.Run away from home

35.Engaged in fights

36.Teasing other children

37.Leader, bossy

38.Difficulty waking up

39.It was a follower, conducted too

40.Difficulty seeing things from someone else's point of view

41.Problems with authorities, school visits to the principal's office

42.Problems with the police

Medical problems as a child

43. Headaches
44. Stomach pains
45. Constipation prison
46. Diarrhea
47. Some food allergies
48. Other allergies
49. Enuresis

As a child at school I was (or had)

50. In general, an average student
51. In general, a poor student, slow learning
52. It took me a while to learn to read
53. Slow reader
54. Difficulty reversing the letters
55. Spelling problems
56. Problems with math and/or numbers
57. Bad calligraphy
58. Able to read very well, but never really liked to read
59. Did not reach the expected potential
60. Repeated low notes
61. Suspended or expelled

25 ADHD-Related Questions

3. Concentration problems, easily distracted
4. Concerns, anxiety
5. Nervous, restless

6. Inattentive, "dreamed awake"

7. Boiling point, "low or high" temperature

9. Explosive temperament, anger accesses

10. Difficulty with persistence to finish the things that began

11. Stubborn, stubborn

12. Sad, unhappy or depressed

15. Rebellious, disobedient and sassy with my parents

16. Low opinion on myself

17. Irritable

20. Mood changes, high and low in temperament

21. Brava

24. Acting impulsively, without thinking

25. Tendency to be immature

26. Feelings of guilt, of repentant

27. Losing control of myself

28. Tendency to be or act irrationally

29. Unpopular with other children, I did not keep friends for long, I did not relate well to other children

40. Difficulty in seeing things from someone else's point of view

41. Problems with authorities, school visits to the principal's office

As a child at school I was (or had)

51   In general, a poor student with slow learning

56. Problems with numbers, calculations and mathematics

59. Not reaching the expected potential

How to Evaluate

The sum of the 25 **ADHD-related** questions is used to calculate a summary **ADHD** score. Because the Wender Utah Evaluation Scale does not separately classify the **ADHD** (presentation specifiers) subtypes. The **ADHD** summary score cannot be integrated with other subtype scores.

WURS Subscore = ___________ (sum of 25 **ADHD**-related questions)

A score below 50 indicates that **ADHD** symptoms are not consistent with a positive diagnosis for attention deficit.

A score greater than or equal to 50 indicates that **ADHD** symptoms are consistent with a positive diagnosis for attention deficit.

The summary score increases as the severity of **ADHD** responses increases. The summary score, therefore, is calculated by adding the answers to the 25 **ADHD**-related questions and using a cutoff of 46.

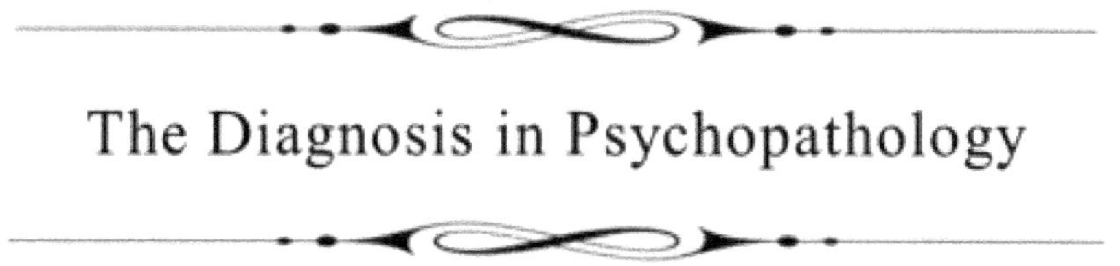

The Diagnosis in Psychopathology

"The descriptive psychiatrist is primarily interested in how similar a patient is, rather than how different it is from other patients with congruent aspects." (GABBARD, 1998).

According to Dalgalarrondo (2000), the study of mental illness begins by careful observation of its manifestations. Observation is physiologically articulated with the ordering of phenomena; this assumes that in order to observe, we need to produce definitions, classifications, interpret and sort by observing it from a certain perspective, according to a certain logic.

We can identify two extreme diagnostic positions: one that states that the diagnosis has no value, because each person is a unique and unclassifiable reality. In this case, the diagnosis would have the function only of labeling different people, eccentric, allowing medical power and social control over the misfit or questionable individual (pure diagnosis). The other position says that the diagnosis is essential in the evaluation of mental pathologies, because observing the singular and subjective aspects of the individual is very important, but without an in-depth psychopathological diagnosis one cannot understand patient and his suffering, nor choose the most appropriate type of therapeutic strategy.

In human nature, three groups of phenomena can be distinguished in relation to their possibility of classification:

1) Aspects and phenomena that we find in all human beings: this group of phenomena is part of a wide category that is too much for classification, being not useful for it. Phenomena such as deprivation of sleep hours causes drowsiness; food restriction causes hunger; that is, they are notorious phenomena, common to all, that do not arouse much interest to psychopathology and are trivial.

2) Aspects and phenomena that we find in some people, but not in all: these are the phenomena of greatest interest for diagnostic classification in Psychopathology, where most signs, symptoms and mental disorders are located.

3) Aspects and phenomena that we find in only one human being in particular: such phenomena, although of interest to the understanding of the human being, are too restricted and difficult to classify and group, having greater interest in their anthropological aspects, existential and aesthetic than properly taxonomic (classificatory).

In confluence with the diverse concepts, through the paradox proposed by Lantéri-Laura (1998) when considering Psychopathology as a subjective phenomenon that is processed between the psychology of the pathological and the pathology of the psychological – it is also verified, the relevance of Semiology and its observational techniques. In this respect, Dalgalarrondo (2000) elucidates the difference between Semiology and Semiotechnical:

a) **Semiology** is the science of the signs, being present in all human activities that include interaction and communication between two interlocutors by the use of a system of signs (speeches, gestures, attitudes, nonverbal behaviors, etc.). It is dedicated to the study of symptoms and signs of diseases, allowing the health professional to identify physical and mental alterations, order the observed phenomena, formulate diagnoses and establish treatment methods.

b) **Semiotechnic,** in turn, refers to specific techniques and procedures of observation, collection and description of signs and symptoms. Thus, it is of essential importance for the practice of Semiotechnics in Psychopathology, the thorough, attentive and insightful observation of the patient's behavior, the content of his speech and his/her way of speaking, his mime, posture, clothing, the way he reacts and his style of relationship with the interviewer, with other patients and his/her family members.

> Medical semiology means the study of symptoms and signs of the disease, which allows the health professional to identify physical and mental alterations, order the observed phenomena, formulate diagnoses and undertake therapies. In general, semiology, or semiotic, is the science of signs. The sign is a type of signal, such as in medical semiology, fever can be a sign/sign of an infection or inflammation. Therefore, the signs of greatest interest for Psychopathology are the objective behavioral signs, the subjective experiences reported by the patient and their complaints. (DALGALARRONDO, 2000).

However, in general, there are basic guidelines in the authors studied that the doctor should follow in order to obtain the information necessary to diagnose and indicate the most appropriate treatment. Among these guidelines, Swales (1990 apud PEREIRA, 2010) highlight:

1) **Psychic Examination**: from which the physician analyzes the psychic functions of the patient, the current mental state, such as presentation of the patient, including hygiene, attitude towards the interview (cooperative, suspicious), characteristics of speech and thought, among others;

2) **Psychopathological Summary**: where the doctor catalogs all psychic functions and their alterations. However, before starting psychopathological examination, there are the 'initial phases' of interaction between doctor and patient, which includes, among other information, the main complaint, the history of the current disease and family history.

In the script of psychiatric interviews, for example, some very common topics are found. These are issues that provide relevant information for the doctor to know the patient, since the interview is intended to give clarity to certain patterns characteristic of the patient's life, and the proposal is to help him in his mental suffering. It is from careful observation that the doctor makes of the patient during the interview that he can confirm or refute the diagnostic hypothesis. Among these topics are foreseen:

a) Initial Schooling;

b) Sexual Preference;

c) Alcohol and Narcotics Use;

d) Attitude towards Loneliness;

e) Attitude Towards the Body;

f) Sleep and Sleep Functions;

g) Leisure Interests.

Due to the important role that the interview plays in the activity of the clinic, a reflection on the scripts is fundamental, since it is from these different orientations that physicians will behave discursively during the interview. It is necessary, therefore, that they know these scripts, and know how to evaluate them so that these orientations can contribute to these professionals in their clinical practice, with a view to understanding the other, meeting the one who seeks relief for suffering Mental. And a possibility of analyzing this discursive-interactional behavior in the 'here-now' of the communicative event can be made from the frames that the doctor establishes during the encounter with the patient. On this, Nunes Filho et al. (2000 apud PEREIRA, 2010) clarifies that the following items are usually present, among others:

a) Medical-Psychiatric Examination, which includes Examiner Presentation, Patient Identification, Main Complaint, Reason for Consultation or Hospitalization, History of Current Disease, Personal History and Family History;

b) Psychopathological Examination (general attitude, thought, consciousness, attention, concentration is some 'topics');

c) Somatic Examination;

d) Complementary Tests: psychological tests and laboratory tests;

e) Syndromic Diagnosis;

f) Hypothesis(s) Diagnostic (s).

The evaluation of the patient in psychopathology is made mainly through the interview. She can't be seen as something banal, a simple ask the patient about some items in her life. The interview, together with careful observation of the patient, is, in fact, the main instrument of knowledge of psychopathology. Through a well-conducted interview with art and technique, the professional can obtain valuable information for clinical diagnosis, to know the affective dynamics of the patient and – what is pragmatically more important – for a better intervention and therapeutic planning. (DALGALARRONDO, 2000).

The area developed by clinical psychology, called Psychodiagnosis represents an important means of aid in psychopathological diagnosis, and for the most part, are made possible through the application of projective, psychometric and personality tests, or also by testing trackers of possible organic changes, as well as more specific neuropsychological tests aimed at detecting cognitive alterations. Complementary tests: complementary laboratory, neurophysiological and neuroimaging tests are also a fundamental aid to psychopathological diagnosis. The mastery of the technique of conducting interviews is what qualifies the skilled professional, being a fundamental and irreplaceable attribute of the health professional.

The interviewer's ability, at first, is revealed by the questions he asks, by those he avoids formulating and by deciding when and how to talk or just shut up and listen. The professional who conducts the interview should also establish an empathic relationship and at the same time useful from a human point of view, besides knowing how to welcome and hear the suffering of the individual, listening to the patient in his difficulties and idiosyncrasies (a way of being to see, feel and react from each one). In addition to patience, respect and empathy, the professional needs a certain temper (moderation, balance) and ability to establish limits to invasive or aggressive patients, and thus protect themselves and protect the content of the interview. (DALGALARRONDO, 2000).

> Through the psychopathological interview, we come to two main aspects of the evaluation: Anamnesis, that is, the history of the symptoms and signs/signs that the patient has presented throughout his life, his/her personal and family antecedents, as well as his family and social environment. Psychic Examination, or Mental Status Exam. Both are more relevant aspects about the technique of interview in psychopathology, but we cannot disregard a physical evaluation, because the physical examination of the patient with mental disorders, when performed properly, can be an excellent instrument of affective approximation, especially in many patients regressed. In addition, the physical examination of the patient with a psychiatric disorder does not differ from that of patients without mental disorders; but often a physical evaluation is made by general practitioners, who in turn do not hear the psychiatric patient as they should be heard, as a result of the stigma of "madman" who invalidates their somatic complaints. We can also, in addition to physical examination, refer the patient to a Neurological Evaluation, where he can help in psychodiagnosis. (DALGALARRONDO, 2000).

The initial interview is considered a crucial moment in the diagnosis and treatment of mental health. This first contact, when well conducted, should produce in the patient a sense of confidence and hope in relief of their suffering. Otherwise, when initial interviews are found and disastrous, in which the professional is unintentionally or not negligent or hostile, they are followed most of the time in the abortion of treatment.

At the initial moment, the look, and with it, all his nonverbal communication, already has its substantial value, because it is in it that the whole emotional burden of being seen, of gesture, posture, clothing, smiling or expressing his feelings is included. This first contact and the first impression that the patient produces in the interviewer is actually the product of a mixture of many factors, such as clinical experience, transfer and countertransference and personal values and inevitable prejudices that the whether you like it or not, carries with you. Early in the interview, it is convenient for the professional to present himself, saying his name, profession, specialty and, if applicable, the reason or reason of the interview. Confidentiality, privacy and confidentiality can be explicitly guaranteed if you notice the shy or suspicious patient. Therefore, it is of fundamental importance to make clear to the patient the confidentiality and description of the interview and that they will be broken in the case of seriously self-or-destructive ideas, plans or acts. (ibidem).

Sometimes a well-conducted interview is one where the professional speaks little and listens a lot to the patient, other times, the situation requires that the interviewer be more active, talking more and asking more questions. This varies greatly and function:

a) **Of the patient**; his personality, his mental and emotional state. Sometimes the interviewer needs to hear a lot, because the patient needs to talk a lot, vent. Other times, the interviewer should speak more, so that the patient does not feel too shy or withdrawn;

b) From the institutional context of the interview, that is, where this interview will be held, in an emergency room, infirmary, outpatient clinic, etc.

c) Of the objectives of the interview, if it is being performed for a clinical diagnosis, establishment of therapeutic bonds, forensic issues, etc.;

d) From the interviewer's personality, that is, some professionals are great interviewers talking little during the interview, being discreet and introverted; others, but only manage to work well and conduct good interviews, being spontaneous, talking and extroverted.

Dalgalarrondo (2000) also highlighting some negative points that should be avoided by the professional during the interviews:

a) Rigid and stereotyped postures, which are formulas that the professional deduces that would work well with some patients and therefore should work with everyone. Therefore, the professional should seek a flexible attitude that adapts to the personality and symptoms of the individual, as well as his culture, ideology and personal values;

b) Excessively neutral or cold attitude, which transmits to the patient often a situation of distance and contempt;

c) Overly emotional or artificially warm reactions, which produce a false intimacy. What should be done is to create a relationship of respect and consideration for the patient, but in a genuine way, without extreme coldness or exaggerated caution;

d) Valuable comments or judgments about what the patient reports, feels, experiences or presents;

e) Intense emotional reactions of pity or compassion, as a desperately upset patient benefits much more from a professional who welcomes such suffering in an empathetic way than a professional who despairs of him;

f) Respond with hostility or aggression to hostile attacks or aggressiveness of the patient. The professional should make it clear that the patient is being inadequately hostile and that, although in a serene and soft tone, he must make it clear that he will not accept exaggerated physical or verbal aggressions, because such behaviors and discussions are usually useless or negative in contact with the patient;

g) Overly prolix as interviews (too long or diffuse; boring), but deep down it says nothing substantial about their suffering. When this occurs, the professional should have the ability to conduct the interview for more significant points and terms,

h) Making many notes during the interview, because this behavior adopted by the interviewer can transmit to the patient that the notes are more important than the interview itself, so it is fundamentally important to observe whether the act of making notes bothers the patient.

The important thing is, above all, to point out that although the professional has only between five and ten minutes to serve a patient in these institutions, he should examine the same with patience and respect, creating an atmosphere of trust and empathy, even with the time constraints, because it is often not the amount of time or interviews that the professional has with the patient, but the quality of care that the professional can offer the patient is that it can generate a better quality in care. (DALGALARRONDO, 2000)

> The professional with some experience in Psychopathology, however, can detect that the data of an interview may be being underestimated or overestimated. Because sometimes the patient denies having the symptoms, to impersonate a "normal" person, without any disorder. This is called concealment, which is the act of voluntarily hiding or denying the presence of psychopathological signs and symptoms. Such a negative occurs for fear of possible hospitalization, taking psychiatric medications or simply being listed as "crazy" or "mentally ill". However, on the other hand, we have the simulation process, which, unlike concealment, is the attempt to create, voluntarily present a symptom, sign or experience that does not really have, that is, he says listen to voices, feel psychosomatic pain, of being emotionally unbalanced always in order to get something like: retirement, work dispensation, not go to jail, or many other factors that can be avoided with a diagnosis of mental illness. (ibidem).

One of the most frequent methods of mental illness classification is by categorizing experiences described by mentally ill people and defining the terms used, such as "depression" or "anxiety". For progress in prognosis and treatment, such classification is essential. When trying to understand the subjective experiences of a suffering person, the therapist demonstrates involvement and the patient will probably have greater confidence in the treatment. Symptoms are aggregated by certain patterns and we can therefore speak of different mental or psychiatric diseases. Precise diagnostic methods or the definition of the nature of the problem remain important. In order for psychiatric nosology to be improved, an accurate observation of the phenomena with which we are confronted is necessary. (SIMS, 2001).

But, after all, what is a person obviously affected by a mental illness really feeling? How do your own experiences resemble or differ from the experience of others of both those who are well and from those who are sick? How can we use the word observer with respect to someone else's internal experience? This is exactly where the empathy process. Through these questions, Sims (2001) points out that listening and observing are crucial to understanding. One should be very careful when asking questions. Doctors often identify symptoms incorrectly and make the wrong diagnosis because they asked for want questions with which the patient, through his submission to the doctor's status and anxiety to cooperate, is completely willing to agree. The empathy method means using the ability to feel in someone else's situation, advancing through organized series of questions; repeating and reiterating where necessary until you are sure of what is being described by the patient.

Therefore, it is important to try to achieve the subjective meaning of the patient and not only to be satisfied because the response is abnormal. Phenomenological significance is sometimes revealed in the type of response; for example, when asked for a schizophrenic patient to explain the difference between a wall and a fence, he replied, "You can see through a fence, but the walls have ears." In the same way that external events have causes that can be explained, internal psychological events can originate from each other in a significant thread, if the patient's internal state can be understood empirically. (RAWNSLEY 1985 apud PEREIRA, 2010).

Starting from the premise that behavior means something, that is, that arises with internal consistency, from psychic events. Although a patient's behavior may be significant for him, it may not be possible for us, external observers, to understand him. There are many levels in which we can understand. For example, we may have some understanding of the sexual difficulties of a repeat exhibitionist when learning about his troubled childhood; but this is not yet explained why he regularly repeats the behavior that makes him conflict with the law, harming him socially and his family. Wittgenstein (1953 apud SIMS, 2001) stated, "We explain human behaviors giving reasons, not causes." In this sense, Jaspers contrasted compression (verstehen) with explanation (erklären) and showed how these terms can be used in both static and genetic sense. Static means understanding or explaining this situation from the information available; genetic status, as it reached this state by examining its antecedents. As illustrated in **Table 1.**

	Understanding	**Explanation**
Static	(1) Phenomenological Description	(3) Observation through external sensory perception
Genetic	(2) Empathy established from what emerges	(4) Cause and effect of scientific method

Table 1. Diagram of understanding and explanation.

According to Giorgi (2006 apud FEIJOO, 2016) understanding is the perception of the personal meaning of the patient's subjective experience:

1) If we want to find meaning at a certain time in time, the phenomenology method is appropriate. The subjective experience of the patient is dissected forming a static picture of what such thought or such an event meant to him at that given moment. No comment is made on how the event came about and no prediction to what will happen next. The meaning is simply drawn as a description of what the patient is experiencing and what this means to him now. A man feels angry: static understanding uses empathy to describe in detail exactly how it is for him to feel angry. I, the examiner, have I experienced phenomena like these? Are they known to me for the experiences I've had in my life?

2) Genetic understanding, as opposed to static comprehension, is concerned with a process. It is understood that when insulted, this man reacts with violence; when this woman hears voices commenting on her actions, she closes the curtains of her house. To understand the way psychic events, originate one of the others in the patient's experience, the therapist uses empathy as a method or tool. He puts himself in the patient's situation. If this first event had occurred with him in the total circumstances of the patient, the second event, which was the reaction of the patient to the first, occurred within the expected, with some margin of certainty. He understands the feelings attributed to the patient from the action that results from them. So, if I were the patient with the same story, would I have the same experiences and the same behavior? An example would help demonstrate the humanity of this approach and the universality of human experience: I must put myself in the shoes of a young 19-year-old woman raised in an isolated fishing community, the oldest of eight children, who becomes stupors during her second pregnancy. She is married to a 35-year-old alcoholic man, and her father is also an alcoholic. I must understand how she handled her father's behavior as a child; what her pregnancy meant to her; as she saw her mother's behavior during her pregnancies, etc. The explanation deals with the record of events from an observation point outside of these;

understanding, from within them. It is understood the anger of a person and its consequences; the occurrence of snow in winter is explained. Explanations can also be described as static or genetic.

3) Static explanation refers to external sensory perception, observation of an event.

4) The genetic explanation consists of the discovery of causal connections: it describes a chain of events and why they follow this sequence. Understanding and explaining are necessary parts of psychiatric research.

In his book, *Psychopathology and Semiology of mental disorders,* Dalgalarrondo presents two tables: Initial evaluation and introductory questions and psychiatric history. In the first, there are general guidelines on what should be the doctor's conduct during the interview:

a) Provide a place with a minimum of privacy and comfort for the interview;

b) Introduce yourself to the patient and then briefly explain the objective of the interview;

c) Establishing an empathic contact with the patient, start with the general questions about who the patient is: What is the (a) lord (a) called? How old are you? "What's your marital status"? (Basic Sociodemographic Data), among other recommendations.

In the second picture - Psychiatric History - there are 14 subtopics that make up the interview itself. Some of them are Identification, Main Complaint and History of Current Disease, Habits, Relationship and Family Dynamics, Results of complementary evaluations, Diagnostic hypotheses and Therapeutic planning and therapeutic actions implemented, among others. For all subtopics, however, there are gaps that must be filled by the doctor with the information provided by the patient. For example, in relation to the Main Complaint and History of Current Disease, the guidelines are as follows:

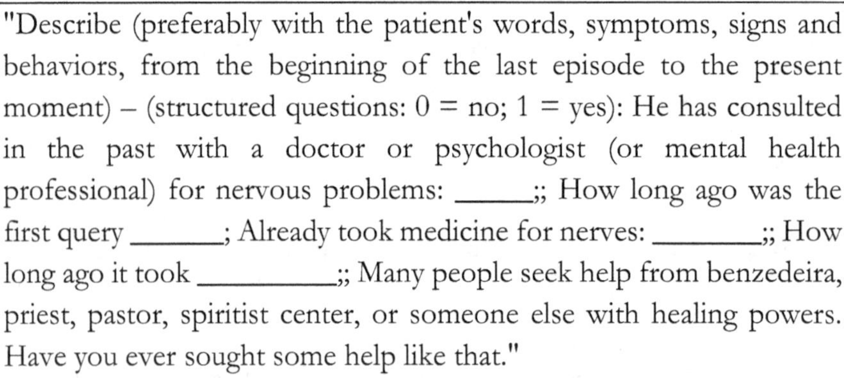

"Describe (preferably with the patient's words, symptoms, signs and behaviors, from the beginning of the last episode to the present moment) – (structured questions: 0 = no; 1 = yes): He has consulted in the past with a doctor or psychologist (or mental health professional) for nervous problems: _______;; How long ago was the first query _______; Already took medicine for nerves: _________;; How long ago it took ____________;; Many people seek help from benzedeira, priest, pastor, spiritist center, or someone else with healing powers. Have you ever sought some help like that."

Table 2. Instructions for identifying the current and main complaint (DALGALARRONDO, 2000).

In addition to these, other information should be obtained in order to transmit to the doctor a greater number of information on the history of the disease. The script presented by Dalgalarrondo is guided, oriented, following the 'survey model' of obtaining answers — the focus is on the content of the questions, whose answers will inform the doctor about the patient's pathology since the goal is to know the disease. According to this author, in order for the patient to express signs and symptoms, the doctor should be aware of what he narrates, observing the patient's 'style', his appearance and his basic attitudes. That is, the attitudes and behavior of the patient will be at the service of this objective: to know and treat the disease.

In the script of the psychiatric interview presented by Dalgalarrondo are also included, in addition to Anamnesis, the Psychic Examination and the Psychopathological Summary. Thus, adopting a more instructive posture that tends to conduct the behavior of the physician, universalizing and generalizing the cases, after presenting some pictures, makes several recommendations, also emphasizing certain attitudes that should be taken by the interviewer during the interview so that it does not harm the course of interaction. Two of them clearly represent the model of physician-centered medicine as a specialist, whose conduct should be the reflection of their institutional medical knowledge:

a)   One should avoid terminology by too many technicality who generally reveal insecurity of the professional, who seeks to compensate, in the far-fetched language, the vacuums of his ignorance about the case, or who wants to demonstrate in an exhibitionist way his erudition and know doctor;

b)   It should be remembered that, despite the fact that a psychopathological history is usually described irrational phenomena, often disorganized and chaotic, the report should be organized and coherent, facilitating the establishment of hypotheses diagnostic and appropriate therapeutic planning. The patient has the right to be confused, contradictory, illogical. The professional, when reporting the case, does not have this right.

In Dalgalarrondo's recommendations, the 'roles' that the physician and the patient's disease occupy in the script can be known, demonstrating what conduct the professional should have in order to meet the requirements of this normative model: "the mastery of the technique of performing interviews is what specifically qualifies the skilled professional." Discussions about the role of the patient as a subject of his mental suffering are not expressed.

It is noteworthy that these guidelines proposed by Dalgalarrondo, which are discursive practices, do not point to the importance and consequent insertion of the patient in the interaction, which triggers a more marked instructional aspect, in addition to the consequent control of the doctor about the interview. In fact, the pictures presented by him provide the practical facilitation of less experienced professionals, since the 'model' would already be organized. In principle, these cadres may seem to help the doctor conduct the interview, however, tend to standardize interviews, without taking into account the different patients with their different life stories.

Final Considerations

The World Health Organization (WHO) defines Mental Health as a welfare state in which the individual is able to exercise his skills, manage normal stressful events in life, work productively and contribute to his community. A Mental Disorder, therefore, can be understood as a medical condition that alters this state causing impairment in the individual's overall performance. According to the Brazilian Psychiatric Association (BPA) it is estimated that more than 40 million people in Brazil suffer from some type of mental disorder. Thus, those suffering from Depressive Disorders, Obsessive-Compulsive Disorder (OCD), Hyperactivity Attention Deficit Disorder **(ADHD)**among so many other mental illnesses begin to feel increasingly excluded, in the face of these types of prejudiced manifestations disseminated by the media.

On the existence and veracity of **ADHD,** it is worth noting that — in addition to being officially recognized by the World Health Organization (WHO) — **ADHD** is also validated by an International Consensus: scientific production published after extensive debates among researchers from different cultures, institution, and that they do not necessarily share the same ideas about all aspects of a disorder. According to the American *Psychiatric Association* (1994) **ADHD** is one of the best studied disorders in medicine, and general data on its validity are much more convincing than most mental disorders, and even many medical conditions.

Currently, **ADHD** is the most frequent reason among children and adolescents referred for care in specialized services. It is estimated that it affects 2.5% of adults, about 3 to 7% of school children (from 6 to 12 years old) worldwide, and in more than 68% of cases the disorder remains throughout life. According to the Diagnostic and Statistical Manual of Mental Disorders in its 5th edition **(DSM**-V), **ADHD** is more common in males than in females, in the proportion of 2:1 in children, and 1.6:1 in adults. The characteristics related to inattention have a higher incidence in females, while symptoms related to hyperactivity and impulsivity are more observed in males. The disorder also has high rates of comorbidities: in children with **ADHD**, more than 50% of cases arises with the presence of — at least — some other comorbid disorder, and approximately 10% of them, develop three or more comorbidities. Research indicates that among children, the most frequent are:

- Defiant Opposition Disorder — 40 %

- Anxiety Disorders — 34%

- Conduct Disorder - 14%

- Learning Disorders (Reading, Calculus and/or Writing) - 10 to 25%

- Tic Disorder — 11%

- Mood Disorders - 4%

Among adults with **ADHD,** comorbidities affect approximately 70% of patients — of which 97% have up to four comorbid disorders. Studies indicate that for every five adults undergoing treatment for some other disorder, at least one of them has ADHD. Among the most common comorbidities observed in adults are:

- Depression — 20 to 30%

- Anxiety disorder -20 to 30%

- Substance use - 25 to 50%

- Smoking - 40%

- Antisocial personality disorder - 25%

- Sleep disorder - 75%

In addition to triggering serious losses of productivity and motivation in academic, vocational activities, as well as a reduced ability to express ideas and emotions, instability in different types of relationships, impairment of execution memory, social retracting, negative effects of the image itself, etc. Hyperactivity Attention Deficit Disorder **(ADHD)**usually causes a series of impacts in the course of a person's life:

1) Adults with **ADHD,** regardless of the level of education, earn salaries significantly lower than adults without the disorder. The study showed that the difference is around $10,000 annually for individuals with higher education and 4,000 for those with only high school;

2) 25% of adults with **ADHD** do not finish 2nd grade against 1% of adults without ADHD;

3) Only 15% of adults with **ADHD** attend university against more than 50% of adults without ADHD;

4) Adults with **ADHD** less often complete a University;

5) Adults with **ADHD** less often get full-time jobs than adults without disorder. Item accounts for 17% of the $77 billion of projected losses in the study. Generating economic impact on society;

6) About 25% of students with **ADHD** present learning problems in any of these sectors: oral expression, comprehension, interpretation of texts and mathematics;

7) 30% of children and adolescents with **ADHD** repeat at least one school year, multiple repetitions occur in 21%;

8) 35% of adolescents with **ADHD** drop out of school, 45% are expelled from schools and 21% have classes repeatedly;

9) It is estimated that the emotional development of children with **ADHD** is about 30% slower than that of children without the

disorder. For example, a 10-year-old with **ADHD** operates at a maturity of 7 years. A young 16-year-old driver with **ADHD** has a profile of decisions of an 11-year-old;

10) 65% of children with **ADHD** present challenge behaviors of authority such as verbal hostility and tantrums;

11) Children with **ADHD** are most often victims of head trauma or polytrauma, accidental intoxications and ICU admission due to these medical complications;

12) Children with **ADHD** have a 3-fold higher risk of domestic accidents, 2 times higher than trauma, sutures and hospitalizations and 20% of them are responsible for serious fires in their communities;

13) Increased risk of pregnancy before 18 years of age and sexually transmitted diseases in young people with **ADHD;**

14) Young people with **ADHD** have a 4 times higher risk of causing accidents, 7 times higher than multiple accidents and with victims, and 4 times higher the incidence of fines (due to speeding and not respecting traffic signs);

15) Young people with **ADHD** are at higher risk of substance use, abuse and dependence. In a survey, tobacco use was reported by 50% of young people with **ADHD** against 27% of young people without the disorder, alcohol use 40% versus 28% and marijuana 17% versus 5%;

16) Separation or divorce occurs 3 times more among parents of children with **ADHD** than parents of children without the disorder;

17) 49% of children with **ADHD** have difficulties in relating to other children versus 18% of controls (children without **ADHD**);

18) 72% of children with **ADHD** have conflicts with siblings and other family members against 53% of controls;

19) 48% of children with **ADHD** have ease of adaptation to new situations against 84% of controls;

20) 18% of children with **ADHD** reported having good friends against 36% of controls;

21) 52% of children with **ADHD** need parental help in school tasks against 28% of controls;

22) 26% of children with **ADHD** need the help of parents to get ready to go to school against 16% of controls;

23) Comparative studies show that adults with **ADHD** have more often: drug addiction (or drug addiction), suicide attempt, divorce, unemployment, professional dissatisfaction and social misfit.

About The Writer

Marcus Deminco (Salvador-BA. Set, 28 1976). Brazilian writer and psychologist; Doctor Honoris Causa in Attention Deficit Disorder/ Hyperactivity Disorder; Practitioner and Tutor of Neuro-linguistic programming (NLP); Portal of Psychologists Newsletter Subscriber. Wrote several texts, phrases and thoughts shared on numerous websites and social networks. Author of 'Why read Paulo Coelho?' Praised and shared by Paulo Coelho himself among his readers. Marcus Deminco is author of:

1) Me and My Friend ADD - Autobiography of a guy with Attention Deficit Disorder.

2) The Secret of Clarice Lispector

3) VERTYGO - The Suicide of Lukas (Portuguese Edition)

4) VERTYGO - The Suicide of Lukas (English Edition)

5) Neuro-Linguistic Programming: beginning by the beginning.

6) Messages to Post, Like and Share. Vol. 1

7) Messages to Post, Like and Share. Vol. 2

8) Messages to Post, Like and Share. Vol. 3

9) E-cards text collection. Vol. 1

10) E-cards text collection. Vol. 2

Awards and Tributes

1.1. Author of 'Estafeta Sem Rumo' – Cecilio Barros Barros Pessoa Awards of Anthology – Academy of Letters, Arts and Sciences of Arraial do Cabo - RJ.

1.2. Doctor Honoris Causa in ADHD by the Brazilian Association of Psychosomatic Medicine in recognition of the scientific contribution and social relevance of the book: Me & My Friend ADHD – Autobiography of a guy with Attention Deficit Disorder.

1.3. One of the winners of *Além da Terra, Além do Céu* prize of contemporary Brazilian poetry awarded by Chiado Editora.

Talk to Marcus Deminco

E-mail: marcusdeminco@gmail.com
Website: http://marcusdeminco.com/
Blog: http://marcusdeminco.blogspot.com.br/
Twitter: https://twitter.com/marcusdeminco
Facebook: https://www.facebook.com/marcus.deminco
Pinterest: https://www.pinterest.com/marcusdeminco/
Instagram: @marcusdeminco
Youtube: https://www.youtube.com/channel/UCRu8yfSoLewjuX6GO6o7Nmw
Tumblr: http://deminco.tumblr.com/
Flickr: https://www.flickr.com/photos/143729713@N06/with/28004881736/
GoodReads: https://www.goodreads.com/author/show/7792932.Marcus_Deminco/
Pensador: https://pensador.uol.com.br/autor/marcus_deminco/